BASKETBALL
SLAVE

BASKETBALL
SLAVE

ANDY JOHNSON
HARLEM GLOBETROTTER/NBA
STORY

MARK JOHNSON
with Tracey Michae'l Lewis

JuniorCam Publishing

Johnson, Mark, 1963-
    Basketball slave : the Andy Johnson Harlem Globetrotter/NBA story
    / Mark Johnson with Tracey Michae'l Lewis. -- Mantua, NJ :
    JuniorCam Pub., c2010.
        p. ; cm.
    ISBN: 978-0-615-17330-6

    1. Johnson, Andy, 1931-2002. 2. African American basketball players--Biography. 3. Basketball players--United States--Biography. 4. Harlem Globetrotters--History. 5. National Basketball Association--History. 6. United States--Race relations--History--20th century. I. Lewis, Tracey Michae'l, 1975- II. Title. III. Title: Andy Johnson Harlem Globetrotter/NBA story.

GV884.J62 J64 2009   2009926917
796.323/092--dc22   0908

Junior Cam Publishing
P.O. Box 302
Mantua, New Jersey 08051
(888) 882-1778

www.basketballslave.com

Cover and Interior Design: Barbara Hodge
Co-Author: Tracey Michae'l Lewis
Editing: Mary Jo Zazueta

Printed in the United States of America

In Loving Memory of my Parents
Andrew and Barbara
who taught the art of loving someone other than yourself.

And, to my nephew Ryan,
who never complains and is an inspiration to all of us.

NATIONAL BASKETBALL ASSOCIATION

OLYMPIC TOWER · 645 FIFTH AVENUE · NEW YORK, N. Y. 10022 · 212-826-7000

PENSION COMMITTEE

July 20, 1992

Mr. Andrew Johnson
P.O. Box 1062
Glenside, PA 19038-1062

Dear Andy:

This letter is to confirm our phone conversation of July 10,
1992 regarding your appeal of the Pension Committee's
decision concerning your eligibility for a Pre-'65 pension.

As we discussed, in order to reconsider our decision, we
require documentation to substantiate the fifth year of
eligibility under the Plan.

Upon receipt of this information, we will re-evaluate your
request for benefits.

Sincerely,

Robert Criqui

One of many denial letters after several appeals to the pension committee.

July 20, 1992
Mr. Andrew Johnson
P.O. Box 1062
Glenside, PA 19038-1062

Dear Andy:

This letter is to confirm our phone conversation of July 10, 1992 regarding your appeal of the Pension Committee's decision concerning your eligibility for a Pre-'65 pension.

As we discussed, in order to reconsider our decision, we require documentation to substantiate the fifth year of eligibility under the Plan.

Upon receipt of this information, we will re-evaluate your request for benefits.

Sincerely,
Robert Criqui

July 31, 1992

Mr. Robert Criqui, Vice-President, Finance
The Pension Committee
National Basketball Association
645 Fifth Avenue
New York, NY 10022

Dear Bob:

I received your letter concerning our phone conversation of July
10, 1992 regarding my appeal to the Pension Committee's decision
of my eligibility for my pre-65 pension.

I really don't understand what documents you and the committee
are waiting for in order to substantiate my fifth year in the
NBA. When my son and I met with you and and Meryl Steinberg,
almost five months ago, I showed you a contract that was received
and recorded by the NBA office and signed by the president of the
team, Frank Lane, and also signed by Maurice Povloff, President
of the NBA. At that time, I explained, in person, the situation
in which I was under contract and under that contract, I was
loaned to another professional team that same year and could not
play anywhere else because I was not put on waivers during that
year in question.

I have been trying to explain my situation since April of 1990,
when the committee first denied my request for my pension. Until
April of 1992, I did not have any documented proof that I was
loaned to another team or was not waived under my NBA contract.
When my contract was recovered and reviewed in your office on
April 28, 1992, I was told that a decision of my appeal would be
made within two weeks and I have not yet received a decision
since I was denied on September 1, 1990.

From the time I left your office on the 28th of April of 1992
until now, almost August, I have been asked to obtain all types
of documentation to back up an "NBA contract". I have tried to
comply with all wishes of the NBA committee to help them in
determining a decision concerning my pension.

You have reviewed letters on my behalf by well-respected men in
professional basketball who have been involved in the game for
over 30 years or more. It has been stated how well I played in
the NBA and how I could have played with any team in the NBA. It
has also been stated in a letter to the committee what actually
happened in the 1962 "loan deal"; also, I was not waived.

Since the committee has received all of this information, I do
not know what else they are waiting for at this time. At this
point, I feel as though the NBA Pension Committee has not only a
legal, but moral obligation to give me an answer concerning my
pension.

Sincerely,

Andrew Johnson

Contents

THE *World* IS THEIR PLAYGROUND-

Acknowledgments

THIS BOOK IS DEDICATED to individuals from all ethnic groups who have been exploited and who never received proper acknowledgment or compensation for their contributions—whether it was building empires or constructing historical buildings.

It is also dedicated to the African-American male sports pioneers:

Before Jackie Robinson made his debut in 1947, playing in Major League Baseball with the Brooklyn Dodgers, Moses Fleetwood Walker was a catcher for the Toledo Mudhens of the American Association in 1883. At that time, few catchers used any equipment, including not wearing a baseball glove for protection.

Willie O' Ree, who broke the color barrier in 1958 to become the first black player in the National Hockey League.

Charles Follis, the first professional black football player to sign a contract (September 16, 1904), and Ollie Matson, who was such a talented and valuable football player that the Los Angeles Rams exchanged nine players for him in 1959.

John Shippen, Jr., golf's first black professional; and Lee Elder, who was the first black golfer to play in the Masters Tournament.

It is also important that we remember the men whose voices went unheard, who were more or just as talented and yet were unable to get the opportunity to play.

Yes, we celebrate Jackie Robinson and all of the *firsts*—the men who paved the way for multi-billion-dollar sports industries. My father, Andy Johnson, was one of those men. Though treated as a slave, *he refused to stay on the bench* and continued to make an impact. He stayed in the game we call life.

In spite of the obstacles, he and others overcame.

Foreword

KNOWING THE HISTORY AND THE IMPACT of black basketball is pivotal in understanding the contributions and struggles of the Original Harlem Globetrotters and the development of the NBA as we know it today.

Dr. James Naismith invented the game of basketball in 1891 because he wanted to create an activity that could be played inside during the winter months. One of the first basketball games ever played was at a YMCA in Springfield, Massachusetts. The game took off—but in different directions. One direction was under Dr. Naismith, who was a sports coach. He introduced the game to colleges. At that time, there was not a high enrollment of blacks in colleges or universities. The other direction went the non-collegiate route. The YMCA exposed communities throughout the country to the game, and these communities were made up of people from different ethnic backgrounds. The YMCAs were a major influence and responsible for the growth and the popularity of basketball. By the end of the century, the first collegiate games were being played for competition.

In New York, the St. Christopher Club (a church program) for young African Americans was also being exposed to this new sport. In the beginning of the 1900s, the surge was on and the game quickly grew to include amateur sports clubs, colleges, and professional clubs all over the country. One of the professional leagues that organized was the New England League, in which Harry Haskell "Bucky" Lew was recorded to be the first African American to play in a professional basketball game in 1902.

In 1904, Edward Henderson, a Harvard-educated physical education teacher from Washington, D.C., introduced the game to young African-American students. He believed the sport would break down segregation and he wanted to promote health, physical fitness, and academic success to build character. And, these young athletes would prove their equality once and for all, thereby diminishing the myth of black inferiority. His efforts went on to create the CIAA which is equivalent to the Big Ten of Black college basketball.

This era was termed the "beginning of basketball" in the book *Hot Potato* by Bob Kuska. The author breaks the history of the sport down perfectly: "The Era of Amateurism, 1910 to 1918; Decline of Amateurism, 1919-1923; and the Rise of Professionalism, 1923-1930. There was no organization of teams across the country. These actions lead to the early professional and barnstorming teams throughout the 1920s. There were hundreds of men's professional basketball teams in towns and cities all over the United States. Part of this barnstorming era

were dominating teams
from New York like The
Original Celtics (all-
white) and two African-
American teams, the New
York Renaissance Five
(Rens) and the Original
Harlem Globetrotters.

Before the dominat-
ing era of the Harlem
Rens, there were a few
teams that made history.
The New York Celtics,
for the first time in
history, would play
an all-black team by the name of the Commonwealth Five.
The Commonwealth Five was owned by two white men,
Roderick "Jess" McMahon and his brother Eddie McMahon.
The Commonwealth Five would go on to win the Colored
Basketball World's Championship, becoming the only white-
owned team ever to win the title. We must not forget about the
all-black Loendi Big Five of Pittsburgh; they also won several
championships. The Savoy Big Five out of Chicago had several
notable wins over the Loendi Big Five. They would eventually
become the birth of the Harlem Globetrotters.

Things changed rapidly when the New York Renaissance
Big Five stepped onto the scene. The owner, Robert Douglass,
a former player and native of the Caribbean, had sole ownership of this all-black team. They separated themselves quickly
by being the first team that was fully black owned. He gave his

players a guaranteed year-long contract, which was not happening at that time. Bob named the former team (Spartan Braves) after the Harlem Renaissance Casino and Ballroom. In 1925, the new Harlem's Renaissance Big Five went on to win the Colored Basketball World Championship.

The Rens provided an opportunity for African Americans to compete against white clubs such as the New York Celtics and Philadelphia Spahs. At some of these events, race riots would break out. Games were sometimes played on a court that was surrounded with chicken wire, thus the term Cage. This was done to prevent bottles and other debris from hitting the players if the home team's crowd did not like the way the game was going. The Rens took on anybody that would play, from black colleges, amateur, to other professional teams.

The Rens dominated basketball for the years that they were on the scene. One year, the Renaissance won 88 straight games in 86 days. They would later go on to win the 1939 World Professional Championship held in Chicago. The Harlem Globrtrotters also played in the tournament but were in the same bracket as the Rens. So those two teams would have never met for the championship. The final score of that tournament championship would be the New York Rens 34 and the Oshkosh All-Stars 25. The Oshkosh All-Stars were a member of the all-white NBL (National Basketball League) precursor to the NBA. That 1938 Championship team consisted of players like John "Boy Wonder" Isaacs, Tarzan Cooper, We Willie Smith (recently inducted into the baseball hall of Fame in 1994 posthumously for journalism), William "Fat's" Jenkins, Eyue Saitch, Zack Clayton, Puggy Bell (MVP), and stand out William "Pop" Gates. Legendary UCLA coach John Wooden stated, "The Rens are the greatest team I ever saw."

Of that championship team, Pop Gates was the only pro basketball player to appear in the World Professional Basketball Tournament at Chicago Stadium for all ten years, from 1938 to 1948. Pop joined the Rens in 1938; he was already on the road to making history. His resume reads like a true legend of basketball. He was the "first" in many accomplishments of the professional era of basketball: from being the first player to jump from high school to appearing in the Pro-World Championship in Chicago; to several All-Pro teams; Hall of Fame teams; and being one of the first blacks to play in the all-white NBL with the Buffalo Bisons, otherwise known as the Tri-City Blackhawks. Pop became the player/coach for the Dayton Rens (formally the Harlem Rens) the only all-black team that was allowed to enter the NBL; he actually had a high-point scoring game of 38 points that year. This was the only black-owned franchise in Major League history—then and now! The firsts did not stop there. Pop went on to become the first black player with the Scranton Minors team in the Eastern League. Pop ended his career with the Harlem Globetrotters, first as a player and then as a coach. He was inducted into the NBA Hall of Fame. Unfortunately, it wasn't until sixty years later in 1989, long after that World Championship game in 1939.

I had rare access to Mr. William "Pop" Gates' last unaired interview in 1998, when he talked about his life and his long career in basketball and being the first of all of these segregated teams in that era. The treatment he had to endure being black and just doing what he was good at was unbelievable. All I can say is that Pop is one of the strongest individuals I know. It was as if he was a one-man civil rights movement by himself. From his inner strength and morals and the help of some of his teammates, players and team owners, he made it through. One of the questions asked of Pop during the interview was: "In all of your years of being around the game of basketball, what is the best Globetrotter team you ever saw?"

He replied, "That period of time of playing, observing, and coaching from the late thirties up to 1955. There were two teams that stand out. The first was the 1939 World Championship Harlem Globetrotter team. This team consisted of players such as Bernie Price, Duke Cumberland, Ermer Robinson, Louis "Babe" Pressley.

The other was the 1956 Harlem Globetrotter team that I had the pleasure of coaching and help assembling. This team consisted of Roman Turman, Willie Gardner, Meadowlark Lemon, Clarence Wilson, Carl Green, Charlie Hoxie, Leon Hillard, Woody Saulsbury, and Andy Johnson."

William "Pop" Gates

Introduction

THERE ARE MANY PEOPLE WHO, when asked about their heroes, quickly and decisively mention an unparalleled athlete, a leader in their community, or a man or woman whose life has made a personal impact on them in some way. People are often influenced by the perceived character of the person and in some cases, the person's ability to succeed against the odds.

The man I have admired my entire life, was in fact, all of the above. He was an unparalleled athlete, an original member of the Harlem Globetrotters, and the third African American to enter the National Basketball Association (NBA) as a Trotter in the 1950s. He was a pioneer and leader in the global community as well as his own. He impacted many people's lives, especially mine. He happens to be my father, Andy Johnson.

My father and I were close. My childhood friends often told me, "I was always envious of you and your father's relationship. But I could never get mad because your dad was like my dad, too."

My father was born in 1931, and many people assume I exaggerate the prejudice he experienced in his early life. I do not. In the online Miriam Webster's Dictionary, *slavery* is defined as the state of being under the control of another person or work done under unacceptable conditions for little or no pay—and that is exactly what happened to Andy Johnson in the 1940s, '50s, and '60s. My beloved father was sold as a slave three times in his life. Surprised? So was I.

It's funny because usually when I say that, people stare at me in disbelief, in spite of the fact that slavery is not a foreign concept. Black slavery in America started in 1619 when a Dutch slave trader exchanged a cargo of Africans for food in Virginia. In 1865, slavery was technically abolished when President Abraham Lincoln signed the Emancipation Proclamation; yet, unfortunately, the racist residue of American slavery would serve as a foundation for my father's issues as related to his basketball career.

His situation came to light in 1990, when he asked me to help him fill out paperwork to get an NBA pension. The forms were two simple pages, basically asking for his name, team, and the year(s) he played. I remember thinking at the time how great it was that the NBA was finally giving the older guys who paved the way for today's million-dollar babies their just due. (Later I would find out that the benefits didn't amount to much.)

There are actually three different pensions for the NBA. There is a pension for pre-1965 players, like the great Joe Faulks, George Mikan, Ray Felix, Tom Gola, and 1957 NBA Rookie of the Year Woody Sauldsberry. Another is for post-1965 players, like Larry Brown, Connie Hawkins, and NBA coach Phil Jackson. Then, there are the current NBA pensions.

In my father's case, as a pre-1965 player, he was to receive about $100 for every grueling year played in the league. That is roughly .0002 percent of an average player's $600,000-$700,000 salary on today's NBA teams. In order for a pre-1965 player to be eligible, he had to have played at least five years with the NBA. This is an interesting criterion considering that back then, the average life of an NBA player was only two to four years, and that of an African-American player was even less because they had to fight to renew their contract every year. Nonetheless, while I thought the pre-1965 players deserved more compensation, I did appreciate the fact that the NBA was, at the very least, acknowledging the hard work of players like my father.

We submitted the paperwork. Within a week my father received a letter from the NBA denying him his pension. He was more disappointed than upset. Basketball had impacted him greatly and to be denied such a nominal amount of money from a multi-billion-dollar industry that might not have survived had it not been for players like him, really hurt my father.

It would take nearly two years of letters, telephone calls, and numerous trips to New York and New Jersey to meet with individuals from the NBA pension committee concerning my father's case to partially reverse that decision. After gathering paperwork from their office and other documentation from well-known individuals, the pension committee finally granted my dad part of his pension. Still, the committee refused to give him the retroactive payment that he deserved. (I later spoke with other pre-1965 players and learned that many of them, white and black, had gone through similar incidents.)

It was this experience and the information that I gathered as a result of it that led me to piece together the components of my dad's amazing story. I began working my way backward through all of his personal accounts. I'd never used my dad's status to my advantage before, but I made a choice to do so now, for a greater purpose. As a result, I gained access to the personal testimonies of many great basketball players—men who too many people today don't know existed. I also discovered how prejudice and segregation really played out in the business of basketball.

In talking with past players, to the fans of that era, and with friends Dad acquired along the way, I found that people thought my father was one of the best. At first, I was disturbed by this because whenever I said "Andy Johnson" to anyone who followed basketball in that era they knew who he was. What was more disturbing, though, is that the NBA's pension committee members did not know who Andy Johnson was and did not bother to find out. I wanted to know how and why my dad and others could be treated in this manner.

On behalf of my father, I sent two letters to the NBA; neither of us ever received a response. Following that silence, I began legal proceedings against the National Basketball Association for my dad's retroactive pension. (A pension that many ex-professional ballplayers were left out of and are still fighting for to this very day, at least the survivors from that era.) I didn't do it because Dad needed the money. He didn't. It was the principle. I felt, and still feel, that he deserves it, along with many others who still have not received their due from this multi-billion dollar organization—despite the fact that if it wasn't for their talent and skills the sport might not have the same mass appeal and impact that it has today.

Dad would often say that the players of today are running up and down the court on old skeleton bones. That was his way of expressing his dissatisfaction about the way older players were being treated. (This sentiment was also expressed in a newspaper article in which many of the old-timers were upset when NBA Commissioner David Stern announced the 50 Greatest Players at a press luncheon on October 29, 1996, in New York City.)

At any rate, I was so thorough in my research during the due diligence process that many ex-NBA players wanted me to fight for them, too. I didn't get a chance to do it then, but maybe with this book, I can do it now.

In the exploration of my dad's story, I needed to gather information regarding his early basketball career. I decided to start with his college alma mater, so I called Portland University, where he was named an All-American in basketball. The plot thickened when I received his obviously altered college transcript. There were inexplicable alterations on this official document. I immediately phoned the university to inquire about them. I left several messages with the person who handles this type of inquiry and I never received a response. That same night I talked with my dad, who couldn't believe what I told him about his transcript.

From that point on, I would receive nightly phone calls from Dad and he would say over and over again, "I can't believe that they did this to me and I let it happen." I reminded him that it was not his fault. Dad asked me about the legal proceedings and I told him I would follow up with the NBA and Portland University. The next day we were to meet for lunch to talk about everything I learned.

The following day, Dad was late for lunch. This was unusual, since Dad was never late—something he had learned when playing with the Globetrotters. He also always answered his phone, so when I couldn't reach him, my heart knew something was wrong, even before my head processed the fact. In August 2002, on the same day I was supposed to hear back from the NBA's pension committee, I found my healthy father dead in his home at seventy-one years of age.

Andy Johnson, an Original Harlem Globetrotter great, a significant part of the integration of the NBA as one of the first African Americans to play in the league, an Eastern League All-Star, and the father I loved with every fiber of my being, was gone. Yes, a piece of me died that day because, as his son, my father represented so much more than basketball to me. Although he was flawed in many of the ways that we all are, in my eyes and the eyes of the people who knew him, he defined what manhood truly is.

After accepting that my father and best friend was gone, without people really knowing who he was, I swore on everything I loved that the life he lived, the trials he experienced and overcame, and his legacy would absolutely not die with him.

That is why *his story* must be told!

Main Entry: ¹**slave**
Pronunciation: \ slāv\
Function: *noun*
Etymology: Middle English *sclave,* from Anglo-French or Medieval Latin; Anglo-French *esclave,* from Medieval Latin *sclavus,* from *Sclavus* Slavic; from the frequent enslavement of Slavs in central Europe during the early Middle Ages

Entry: **wage slave**
Function: *noun*
1 : traffic in slaves; *especially* **:** the buying and selling of blacks for profit prior to the American Civil War
2 : a person dependent on wages or a salary for a livelihood

Entry: **slave driver**
Function: *noun*
1 : a supervisor of slaves at work
2 : a harsh taskmaster
3 : a person held in servitude as the chattel of another
4 : one that is completely subservi-
ent to a dominating influence

Definition from the Merriam-Webster Online Dictionary

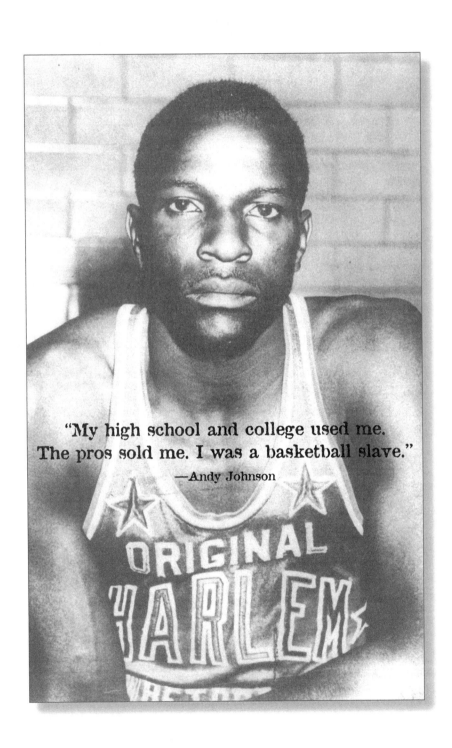

"My high school and college used me.
The pros sold me. I was a basketball slave."

—Andy Johnson

1

The Formative Years

HAVE YOU EVER SEEN A COTTON STALK UP CLOSE? I can recall riding through South Carolina one summer as a teenager and noticing a large amount of cotton growing on either side of the road. Having lived in the North all of my life, the only cotton I was familiar with was the material used to make blue jeans; so I was fascinated by the massive fields I saw that day. Pulling over to the side of the road, I picked a seed from one of the stalks and was surprised to find out that it was like grabbing a hard, prickly, cocoon-like shell. In fact, I had to crack it open like a nut in order to get what looked like a small cotton ball out of the center.

Needless to say, you could easily cut open your fingers if you picked cotton on a regular basis. And, that is exactly what my father's family did for a living in a small obscure town called

Franklinton, floating somewhere in the swamps and bayous of Washington Parish, Louisiana.

The Johnsons were something more than slaves but slightly less than free. Back then it was called *sharecropping*, which most people now know as a legal version of the same atrocity. Sharecropping was a system of farming that developed in the South after the economically destructive Civil War, in which former slave-owners divided their land and crops between themselves and their former black slaves and impoverished whites, who were hired to work the land for a very small wage.

My dad used to tell me about when he was a young boy and his family picked cotton. When they took the cotton to the scales to get it weighed, they were almost always told it weighed less than it actually did. I often wondered why they didn't say anything; why someone didn't try to do something to prevent the fraud from happening.

I realized later that for a black family sharecropping in the Deep South during the 1940s, reading and writing was not an option. The white landowners didn't want their tenants to realize to what magnitude they were cheating them out of their money, and to a certain extent, many of the tenants didn't want to know, either. Knowledge would require responsibility, which would almost always have to turn into action. Not a bad thing, if it wasn't for the fact that, back then, taking action almost always led to death.

My father, Andrew E. Johnson, Jr., was born April 21, 1931, into a large family of eleven siblings. Heading the family were Andy Johnson, Sr. and Betsy Moore Johnson. After enduring the early death of his mother when he was only five years old and the subsequent distancing of his cold and detached father, Dad was left in the care of his oldest sister, Mildred. A pleasant and likable person, she had personality. Her plump figure, along with her firm sweet voice made her a candidate to be anyone's mom, even though she had no children of her own. Mildred was the one who was going to take charge of the family, one by one.

The years between 1910 and 1930 saw a huge migration of blacks from the deep South to urban cites all over the country. This was no exception in the Johnson household. Mildred was the first to leave Louisiana in favor of the sunshine-coated dreams of North Hollywood, California. It was her chance to make a better life for her and her family. When she first arrived in Los Angeles, Mildred Cole worked as a dishwasher at the famous Kay's Drive-In restaurant in North Hollywood. Later she found a job as a maid to the stars of Hollywood's golden film era. As she stabilized herself, she sent for her younger siblings, until most of the Johnsons had been uprooted from Louisiana and settled in southern California. At twelve years old, my father got his chance to make the trek west, and he began his new life as the son of my Aunt Mildred and Uncle Carl, her husband. They raised my dad for the remaining portion of his childhood.

"Here came this little black boy to a white town, who'd never been around white people before. I was way too dumb to know that white people were white. Meaning, I knew they were white but I didn't know that some were better than black people. I didn't have a clue that some white people thought they were better because I didn't see them a lot [in Louisiana]."—Andy Johnson

Take a moment to imagine a young black boy from Louisiana, who'd never actually gone to school, spending the crucial years of his adolescence in the all-white neighborhoods of North Hollywood, a stone's throw from the center of the film industry. Seventh grade would be the first time dad would see the inside of a schoolhouse. He always told me he felt like the character in the children's book *The Jungle Book*. Most people will naturally assume that, given the era, the racism and prejudice Dad experienced in California would be, at the very least, overwhelming. But just like in the children's story, Andy learned how to adapt to his surroundings and his surroundings adapted to him. According to Dad, he never experienced the overt racism he had observed in the South while living in North Hollywood. No doubt, it was there.

Race movies were prevalent and blackface (worn by actors like Mickey Rooney, Jimmy Durante, Judy Garland, and Al Jolson) was common. However, it was enacted in ways that a young boy, especially one used to more overt attacks, might not notice. My dad learned early on in California that an even greater prejudice existed in the form of classism. Many of the issues prevalent in his environment were related to the size of a family's bank account rather than their skin color. At least, that's how my dad remembered it. That was one of many lessons Dad would learn from Mildred's husband, Carl Cole.

Uncle Carl was a small thin man and a good provider for the family. He was also a functioning alcoholic, which made him a colorful character, as he was well-known throughout his church and the community. His creative point of view came in quite handy when disciplining my dad.

Due to the enormous gap in income between my dad and his friends, there were many times he saw things he really wanted yet he knew that Mildred and Carl could not afford them. One time he saw a bike that he liked and, being young and slightly mischievous, he stole it. Someone gave a description of the person who stole the bike and, lo and behold, it matched my dad. Unfortunately, being the only black kid in town meant that the police didn't need a lineup to determine who was responsible.

Policemen approached Uncle Carl about Andy's theft. Uncle Carl vehemently defended my dad in front of the cops and swore that Andy wouldn't do such an awful thing. However, when the police and Uncle Carl confronted Dad, he admitted to stealing the bike, and well, let's just say Uncle Carl lost his cool. Nothing happened to my dad, though. The police simply reprimanded him and went about their day—another example of the different world in which he was living.

Nonetheless, my father learned something that day, as he did every day living in Aunt Mildred and Uncle Carl's house. Uncle Carl, in his unique way, taught my dad a number of important things about life. His words and messages would be the tools that would carry Andy through the tough times yet to come.

One convincing, although risky, lesson was about the power of money. Uncle Carl and young Andy were walking down the street one day when Uncle Carl unexpectedly and harshly kicked the man walking in front of them in the rear end. Dad told me he was frightened because he didn't know what would happen to them. The guy turned around and my dad watched the man's face glow red with anger. Suddenly, Uncle Carl pulled out a twenty dollar bill and handed it to the man. The man, who just seconds before had been kicked in the behind by a stranger on the street, looked at Uncle Carl, took the money, and said, "You old crazy fool," and walked away without incident. Uncle Carl turned to my dad and said, "Now, that's the power of money!"

That day, my dad discovered that some people will place themselves in horrible positions and will endure great pain and embarrassment just for money. This, I think, was a pivotal point in his life, when he decided that money would never be a motivating factor in anything that he did. His motto was "It will never be about the money." Ironically, this lesson would be the one in which he'd be continually tested throughout his life.

There were many more experiences dad would glean from Uncle Carl and the years he spent in North Hollywood. The reality was that although racism wasn't as open and blatant for Andy, it did exist behind the smiles and beneath the surface of the pseudo-acceptance he and his family received. In California, it was less about the physical and emotional humiliation and degradation of minorities and more about a subconscious superiority complex that many of the people in town had toward blacks.

Trying to make sense of the contrasting experiences that he had with white people, Dad would often ponder aloud, "What makes a person *white* in America and *European* overseas?" In North Hollywood, Dad, being the optimist, never allowed the attitudes of others to penetrate him or the relationships he forged while living there. I have no doubt, though, that as he grew older he became more aware of it.

One day, Uncle Carl took Dad to a Harlem Globetrotter's game at the Pacific Arena. It was the most fantastic sight Andy had ever seen. This was around the same time as when the Trotters beat the famous NBA World Championship Lakers— not once but twice—in 1949 and 1950. The very next day, Andy started to practice the moves of players like Goose Tatum,

Marques Haynes, and Erma Robinson. These early basketball pioneers were very important to the black community because they gave black kids someone to look up to. Andy already had a natural ability, but after seeing and hearing about the Trotters, he practiced constantly.

When Andy entered high school, he'd already proven himself to be an unstoppable athlete and fierce competitor in the sandboxes and parks of the San Fernando Valley. Even today, many of his friends joke about how whenever Andy Johnson was asked how he learned to play basketball, he would answer that the best way to learn was to play barefoot. I'm sure as they laughed, they probably never stopped to consider that what he was saying was actually true. Aunt Mildred and Uncle Carl could only afford one pair of shoes, which were hard-soled dress shoes. So, whenever Dad played basketball during recess, he would take off his "good" shoes and wear nothing on his feet but the skin he was born with—and that's how he gained the agility and speed that he exhibited later on the court.

During one of these barefoot basketball games, the North Hollywood High School basketball coach spotted Dad, bought him his first pair of sneakers, and immediately added him to the team roster. In fact, Dad said when he put on the sneakers, he got so excited he felt like he could jump out of the gym! There were no sneaker contracts back then and Dad's barefoot basketball was not a gimmick to sell shoes. It simply drew attention to a young boy from Louisiana who knew how to handle a basketball—and it began Dad's lifelong association with the game.

A year after entering North Hollywood High School, Dad was joined by two other black student athletes, brothers Billy and Charles Reed. Billy, the older of the two was a football player and

LEAGUE CHAMPIONS
1949 N. Hollywood Huskies

Bottom row, left to right: Fred Holzer, Jerry Smith, Don Taylor, Bruce Peibeier, Andy Johnson, Joe Letezia. Middle row: Burt Dillard, Unknown, Bob Hosking, Glen Storment, Mike Hibler. Top row: Coach Albro Lundy, Manager Bugsy Regan, Tom Bohn, Terry Morse.

became one of Dad's best friends, even until his death. In fact, it was Billy Reed who saw the fiercely protective side of Dad. For example, Dad and Uncle Billy were taking an evening ride when they noticed that two white guys in a car were following them. Now, as much as he knew racism in California was less obvious, Dad remembered Louisiana, where this same scenario would be the precursor to a lynching. He wasn't going to take any chances. So, he told Uncle Billy he was going to drive around a bit to see if the two men continued to follow them. If they did, he and Uncle Billy were going to jump out of their car quickly and while Billy held one guy, Dad would beat up the other. He figured if he was going to go out, he was going out swinging. Fortunately for Dad and Uncle Billy, the two guys ended up being their teammates and they were able to have good laugh about it.

The Huskies of North Hollywood High School benefited from my dad's natural skill and ball-handling sensibilities on the basketball court, and there is absolutely no doubt about it. When Dad started playing, they started winning. A six-foot, three-inch, 185-pound guard at sixteen years old, Andy Johnson made the 1949 and 1950 All-San Fernando Valley League High School Basketball Team, led the team to the league championship two years in a row, and became the league's player of the year. He was also one of the best prep basketball players in the state of California. He was the lead scorer in the Valley, with 218 points in twelve games, and went on to become third in the entire city. When Dad played for North Hollywood High, there was a significant amount of money generated by the exhibition games the team played on a regular basis. An article by Willis Arrington, a sports editor for the *Valley Times*, said, "Andy will go down in North Hollywood High history as one of their all-time great hoopsters." The truth was, Dad became such a high school superstar inside and outside of the school that praise seemed to follow him wherever he went. In fact, his high school success parallels the career of our era's Lebron James. Just like Dad, when James was a junior in high school, the school was forced to change the venue of its games simply because the gym where the team played could not hold all of the people who came to watch the young phenom.

Eerily similar to James' circumstance is an amazing story that my dad told me about how he received his first car. (When Lebron was a senior in high school his family was questioned about how they acquired a new car. It was suggested that James was receiving money from boosters.) Dad walked to school every day, and each day he'd pass an older woman standing in her yard. One morning, the woman stopped him and said, "You know, I see you walking to school every day. I have something for you. Come by my house on the weekend to run some errands and I'm going to give you something." Dad said he was really nervous because he didn't know the woman and he wasn't sure what she wanted to give him; however, his curiosity got the best of him and he stopped by the woman's house that weekend.

When he arrived at the house, the lady handed him the keys to a canary-yellow 1939 Packard. Yes, the woman *gave* him a car! And, given the leniency of the forties, when it came to gifts for athletes, he was never questioned about it. Dad was so excited to receive the car he felt like his heart would thump its way right out of his chest. Then he realized he didn't have a license or any money for gas. The license problem was easy to solve; gas money was a bit of a challenge. Nonetheless, Dad and Billy Reed would pitch pennies and bet playground basketball games in order to raise the money needed to keep them rolling.

This kind of favor also followed Dad where he didn't go, meaning his classes. I was amazed when I heard that Dad rarely went to class. Dad literally became the school's basketball mascot. He spent his school days roaming the halls or pitching pennies, while no teacher made him do any studying. Every year, as his coach Albro Lundy "helped" him move onto the next grade level, Dad would joke about how he'd *think* about getting some books, but ultimately he would never step foot in the classroom.

This was further evidence that the prejudicial times in which he lived were not as completely veiled as my dad and his friends sometimes led me to believe. Even the articles in the sports sections of the local newspapers indicated that the writers had never had to report on a young *black* star athlete. They often referred to Andy as the Negro Ace, Colored Flash, and Negro Hoopster. That's how they viewed him—not as a student but solely as an athlete and source of entertainment.

Indeed, why would this all-white school sacrifice one iota of their Negro Ace's brainpower on something they felt was as useless to him and his future as an education? They probably thought his mind should be focused solely on bringing home the championship.

It's amazing that no one questioned it. Beyond prejudice, this injustice reflected the greed of those in leadership and their willingness to take advantage of Dad's talent for personal gain.

"The minute they found out I could make them money, they would not teach me. They wanted me to put all of my mind into basketball."—Andy Johnson

Honestly, I won't pass judgment on my family for allowing this to happen. They all made harsh sacrifices. It was the late forties and my aunt and uncle worked long shifts to provide the bare necessities. In order for Aunt Mildred to obtain and keep her "great" job as a maid to the stars, she was forced to have a hysterectomy. This was so she wouldn't get pregnant and miss work. My aunt was never formally educated, so the likelihood of her knowing there was a problem and being able to identify it and having the power to do something about it simply did not exist.

Many people think that the emphasis on sports and the revenues and bragging rights generated by athletic competition *over* the education of student athletes is a new phenomenon; my dad's situation is a primary example that this isn't the case. Of course, back then, the value of an education for a black child was different than it was for a white child. This is pre- *Brown vs. the Board of Education*, before the case brought national attention to the education of blacks in America. However, it would also be ridiculous to place all of the blame on the existence of racism. It was probably more economic and egocentric than anything else.

Dad's presence on the team filled the stands and brought home trophies. Dad used to say to me, "You can tell a player's personality in life by the way he played sports," and that rang true even for himself. Dad was humble and giving, with a strong work ethic. He also had a way of getting into the other teams' players' heads. I remember a story that Mike Hibler, Dad's former teammate and good friend, told me. It was about how Dad would get to the game early and as the other team entered the gym, Andy would be sharpening his knife and looking at each player with the meanest look they had ever seen as they walked by him. It was immediate intimidation. Mike says he would hear some of the opposing team players say, "Stay away from that guy; he's crazy." Or he recalled how right before tip-off, Dad would go to the captain of the opposing team and show him an imaginary box on the court around the basket. Dad would tell the captain that the area belonged to him, and he did not want to see the captain or any of his teammates in that area. These were some of the mind games Dad would play, which kept his teammates laughing and winning. And when the game started and he was on the court, Andy Johnson was known for not only being a strong, consistent, and exceptional player, but for making his team better as well. He sacrificed his own scoring in order to hand off the ball to other teammates. During my dad's tenure, North Hollywood remained a staple in the high school sports sections of all the local newspapers.

One trademark of my father's personality was his ability to make everyone around him feel comfortable. I believe he learned this in high school, when he had to figure out how to find acceptance on an all-white basketball team in a mostly white school in a predominantly white city. As a result, Andy Johnson showed people what they wanted to see in a way that permitted him to maintain his integrity but also allowed him to slip under the radar—a pretty good feat for a black man in the 1940s and 50s. Learning to draw attention away from his blackness was one of my dad's ways of dealing with the situation. Aunt Mildred told him that he must "learn how to behave." My father lived by this simple advice.

The conflicting perspectives of my dad's high school buddies indicate this. Mike Hibler saw a different side of Dad than the others. "They called us the Gold Dust twins. Andy was more white than I was," Uncle Mike said one day.

Maybe in some weird way, this was true. Dad had experienced more by the time he was twelve years old than most children his age, and from that he learned how to adapt to various situations and people. The Hiblers were a prominent family in the Los Angeles area and Mike was often described in newspaper articles as the "skinny kid with movie-star looks." As a result, I think Dad allowed Uncle Mike to see and feel because, in that world, it was easier for both of them. Dad was the basketball star in Hollywood and therefore he could fit in.

The complex and often contradictory times they lived in fed much of the mentalities of both the black and white athletes of the time. While Billy Reed says that not going to class didn't hurt Dad "too much"—because of the opportunities Dad had in spite of that fact—Mike Hibler denies it impacted Dad "at all." While I love both Uncle Mike and Uncle Billy, and I know that without a doubt Dad loved them and their families, I'm pretty sure that if these men looked beyond the good memories, both would see why I disagree with them about the consequences of Dad's class attendance and the evidence of subtle discrimination.

It's ironic when Uncle Mike says, "Not going to class didn't hurt Andy at all," and in the next breath talk about how his playing with Dad helped him go on to play for UCLA. Uncle Mike played for revered coach John Wooden, who wanted to bring my dad to UCLA but couldn't because Dad's "grades weren't good enough." In fact, the Lakers wanted Dad even before they approached the legendary Elgin Baylor, but because he couldn't get into UCLA, Dad's chances of staying in Southern California and playing for that team were slim. Nonetheless, Uncle Mike and my dad saw things differently because of the time period they grew up in. This is probably why they were able to maintain such an excellent friendship.

Years later, Uncle Mike told me that Coach Lundy actually told all of Dad's teachers to pass Dad so that he could play basketball. Coach Lundy was not being malicious. Coach was a kind man who cared for his players. He truly believed basketball was my dad's future. Unfortunately, Coach did not look at the big picture. (Note: Coach Lundy's own son Albro Lundy, was one of the most famous MIA pilots during the Vietnam war.)

Truth be told, I believe in his later years, my dad finally understood the disservice the coaches and administration did to him by allowing him not to get an education. When you are seventeen years old and you can play basketball, pitch pennies, and drink Coke all day at school, both you and your friends think it's the coolest thing in the world. You may sense you're missing out on something, but your maturity level doesn't afford you the opportunity to figure out what. It would take several years, many experiences, a few open doors, and several shut ones, before Dad actually would.

And then my father promised himself that all of his children would go to college and get an education, which we did.

2

Sold! To the University of Portland

WHAT EXACTLY IS THE NEXT STEP for an eleventh-grade, Louisiana-born, black boy in the 1950s, who's never actually attended class? I'm sure many of the answers would be less than positive. Some would say, "Start the twelfth grade and prepare for graduation." However, the next step in Andy Johnson's story is much different than you'd expect: Dad went to college. To be specific, he went to the University of Portland in Oregon. Yes, he went from the eleventh grade to a major university—without a high school diploma.

Sometimes when I think about my father's life, I feel a weird mixture of pride and sadness. I'm proud of my dad for turning each potential obstacle into opportunity and growth; yet I'm saddened by how some people took his future into their own hands for profit and prestige, without thinking or caring about the long-term consequences of their actions.

PORTLAND, OREGON, FRIDAY, FEBRUARY 2, 1951

Can You Guess Why They Call Andy 'Handy'?

IT'S PRETTY OBVIOUS where "Handy Andy" Johnson, University of Portland center, gets that monicker "Handy." Andy and mates meet their traditional rival, Gonzaga, tonight and Saturday night at Portland's Howard hall. Game time is 8:15

Andy was the first African American that attended the University of Portland for basketball. He was responsible for the school's first win over top-ranked University of Oregon.

Was Andy Johnson smart enough to earn a high school diploma? Yes, he absolutely was. He taught himself how to read by picking up the one book that always seemed to be accessible to him: the Holy Bible. Later, on his own, he read books on various philosophers, prophets, and their teachings. When he traveled to the Middle East, he read from the Holy Quran. While in Israel, he read from the Torah. He loved people and learning about them; so while his academic ability lay dormant because of lack of stimulation, the brilliance was there.

I found ways to get around spelling and 'white people' talk. "—Andy Johnson

Dad always said that if someone had told him he wouldn't be able to play high school basketball unless he went to class and kept his grades up, there would have been no question about him attending class. If someone had threatened to kick him off of the team; if the school, as it sometimes happens today, felt like there could be a lawsuit; or maybe if the school just cared enough about his future, there is no doubt that Dad's plight would have been different. But nobody made him learn and as a teenager he did not understand the ramifications of not getting an education.

Around town, Andy played pick-up basketball games in the schoolyard with mostly white guys. Andy would devastate them every time. Astonished, the guys, who were college players, would ask him what college he played for. Dad would tell them that he was only in the eleventh grade. Their astonishment, and later their comments to their own coaches about the exceptional black kid in the schoolyard, led to a house visit from a gentleman. He asked Aunt Mildred and Uncle Carl if Andy could go to the University of Portland. Mildred said he was only in the eleventh grade, but the gentleman replied, "We can work it out."

Before he knew it, Andy Johnson was *sold* to the University of Portland—without obtaining his high school diploma. For Portland, it would be the deal of a lifetime—a steal in more ways than one. Rather like buying a new car that you'll get great mileage out of for at least four years and only pay pennies on the dollar.

A strong statement, I know. But there had to be a financial transaction between the coaches and administration of North Hollywood High School and the coaches and administration of the University of Portland, who were mostly Catholic priests of the highest order, to take a teenager out of high school and send him to a college that was fourteen hours away from his home. All Dad ever said about his move to Portland was that he heard the coaches talking amongst themselves. And, without a school counselor or a career guide to talk with, Aunt Mildred and Uncle Carl thought sending Andy to college was a good thing. What other choice was there? And, like the gentleman said, "We will take care of it." And they did!

***

My initial research into the matter began when Dad told me a few years ago that he didn't have a high school transcript. To say the least, I was shocked. I told him, "Of course you have a transcript. Everyone has a transcript. It's a law." Not that I knew which law it was or what the law actually said; I just figured there was a law written somewhere, in some book, that said everyone who attended high school should have a transcript.

So I decided to prove him wrong by sending off for his high school and college transcripts. Continually he'd say, "You're not going to get anywhere. You're not going to get anything." Well, he was half right. Dad's transcript from the University of Portland clearly states "did not graduate" as his status in high school. When I first read this, I wondered how that happens. How does a four-year Catholic university admit a student without a high school diploma or something equivalent? He didn't even take a test. I wondered if this was a common practice and how many others were plucked from high school based solely on their athletic prowess. How many colleges built their sports programs this way?

Needless to say, it has been several years since my first request and I'm still waiting for his high school transcript.

University of Portland — Permanent Record
PORTLAND 3, OREGON

NAME ___ Johnson, Andrew Jr.
Address ___ 5505 Cleon Ave.
___ N. Hollywood, California

Parents or Guardian ___ Mildred Cole(Guardian)
Address ___ Same

Birth Date ___ Nov. 8, 1931
Entered ___ Sept. 18, 1950
Discontinued ___ Jan. 27, 1953
Re-Entered ___
Degree ___ Date ___

College ___ Liberal Arts ___ Department ___ Physical Educatio
High School ___ N.Hollywood H.S.
City and State ___ Hollywood, Calif.
Date of Graduation ___ Did Not Graduate
RECORD: Eng. 2½; Gen.Math ½; Basic Math 1½;
Sci. 1; W.Hist ½; U.S. Hist 1; Physical Sci. 1;
P.E. 3; Misc. 6

Total: 17 units

OFFICIAL COLLEGE RECORD

Course & No.	DESCRIPTIVE TITLE	Gr	Hrs	Pts	Course & No.	DESCRIPTIVE TITLE	Gr	Hrs	Pts
	1950-51 1st Semester					**1951-52 2nd Sem.**			
PE 131	Personal Hygiene	B	2	6	Biol 104	General Biology	F	3	0
Journ 105	Elem. Journalism	C	3	6	P E 202	Adv P E	A	1	4
PE 307	Coaching of Basketball	A	3	12	P E 421	Ath Train & Condition	A	2	8
Hist 201	United States History	W	-	-	P E 308	Coach Football	A	2	8
PE 101	Elem. Physical Educ.	A	1	4	P E 304	Prin of P E	A	2	8
Psy 101	General Psychology	C	3	6	Phil 212	Main Probs of Phil	D	3	3
			12	34				13/10	31
	1950-51 2nd Sem.					**1952-53 1st Sem.**			
Jour 106	News Writing	D	3	3	P E 427	Adm of Intramural Sport	I/F	2	0
Psy 102	General Psychology	E/D	3	3	Hist 201	Hist of U S	F	3	0
PE 102	Elem. Physical Educ.	A	1	4	Eng 201	Surv of Amer & Eng Lit	E/F	3	0
PE 402	P.E. Activity	I/C	1	2	Psy 481	Criminal Psychology	F	3	0
PE 232	School Health Educ.	C	2	4	Biol 103	General Biology	FA	2	0
PE 306	Coach. Track: Field	I/C	2	4	P E 231	Intro to Health Educ	D	2	2
PE 132	Introd. to Physical Ed.	I/D	2	2				15/2	2
			14	22					
	1951-52 1st Sem.					Cum 70/51 112			
P E 407	Adm of Phys Educ	D	2	2					
P E 201	Advanced P E	A	1	4					
P E 305	Coaching of Baseball	C	2	4					
P E 331	First Aid	C	2	4					
Hist 103	Hist of U S & Institu	I/F	3	0					
Eng 102	Rhetoric & Comp	I/C	3	6					
Psy 211	Psy of Adjustment	D	3	3					
			16/13	23					

TRANSCRIPT ISSUED IN SEALED ENVELOPE

ISSUED TO STUDENT

(CONTINUED ON REVERSE OF THIS FORM)

Explanation: A, Exceptional, 4 honor points; B, Superior, 3 points; C, Average, 2 points; D, Inferior, 1 point; F, Failure, 0 point; FA, Failure because of absences, 0 point; E, Absent from final examination; Inc, Incomplete; W, Withdrawal (with permission). 128 Semester Hours Including 4 Semester Hours Physical Education required for graduation (Minimum). Academic Year divided into two semesters of 18 weeks each.

ENTITLED TO HONORABLE DISMISSAL UNLESS OTHERWISE NOTED.

SCHOLARSHIP SUMMARY

Semester	Sem Hrs.	Hon Pts.	GPA	Cumul GPA
1-23-51	12	34	2.83	
6-3-51	14	22	1.57	2.15
1-22-52	16/13	23	1.43	1.88
6-1-52	13/10	31	2.38	2.00
1-27-53	15/2	2	0.13	1.60

ACADEMIC STATUS

9-18-50 Admitted on Probation
1-23-51 Off Probation
1-22-52 On Probation
6-1-52 Off Probation
1-27-53 On Probation

Roberta D. Lindahl
Registrar

JUN 25 2002

Registrar

A copy of Dad's transcript from the University of Portland. The birth date was made up. His actual birth date was 4/21/31.

***

While Dad's life in Portland sometimes paralleled his life in California, in a number of other ways, Portland was a different ball game altogether. Yes, he was one of the first black students at North Hollywood and the first black ballplayer at the University of Portland, but Dad lived in somewhat of a cocoon in North Hollywood. Black and white people were comfortable with him and his family. They knew him and maybe even cared for him. Even those who weren't thrilled about the integration of *their* neighborhood tolerated Andy Johnson because of his skills on the court. Plus, in California he was surrounded by movie stars who were much more liberal than Middle America would ever be. Dad always claimed to have dated Doris Day and even joked about taking her to the prom. Ms. Day later released a song with lyrics that said "the secret isn't a secret anymore." To hear Andy Johnson tell it, that song was clearly about him.

Nonetheless, leaving North Hollywood exposed Dad to elements that he wasn't familiar with. In Portland, he didn't have the support he did in California. In Oregon, the ugly monster of racism reared its head, posing dilemmas he'd never dealt with before.

Dad began attending the University of Portland in September 1950. It was a far cry from the sunny skies and warm weather in North Hollywood. The climate change was dramatic. Portland had just endured a brutal winter; the entire city had been blanketed by a foot of snow and by midwinter there was a total snowfall of more than forty-one inches and an all-time record temperature of minus two degrees.

There was another significant change in store for Dad. The city was contending with its own racial tensions. The same year he arrived in Portland, the City Council tried to create a commission on inter-race relations, which would investigate problems arising from discrimination. Needless to say, the civil rights ordinance to create this commission was defeated by the general election.

On top of everything, Portland's population was shifting. The city first feared the growing Asian population, but that fear was replaced by the influx of African Americans who, according to an article in the 1945 *Oregonian*, would raise the level of crime and decrease property values. Whites were determined to keep the city segregated. They demeaned the African-American residents, while police shot at blacks for minor crimes.

Portland was definitely not a place for a young Andy Johnson, and the University of Portland wasn't much better. It wasn't until Dad's last year there, 1953, that the Urban League and its supporters were able to get a law passed to outlaw racial discrimination in public places. Although Dad could play and win basketball games for the university he wasn't allowed in most establishments within the city limits.

Dad shared a story about a white guy who walked by him and intentionally stepped on his foot. Dad thought to himself, "What's wrong with this guy?" Then the guy came back around and stepped on his foot again, this time saying, "You ain't nothing but a nigger."

This took a ton of nerve because my dad was a naturally strong and big guy. I can imagine the surge of rage and resentment that reverberated through Dad's body as he picked the guy up by the neck and beat him so badly he could barely talk.

However, when the guy did find the ability to say a few words, he said, "You can beat me all you want, but you're still a nigger."

Dad learned a vital lesson that day, something that he later taught me, my brother, and my sister. He told us that sometimes hatred is so deeply rooted in a person that there is nothing you can do about it. You can't talk it out of them and you sure can't beat it out of them. From that day forward, Dad never allowed words to affect him.

Dad told me he dated a white woman. Although it's hard for me to picture, he said he wore a bonnet on his head to look like a female when calling on her. Again, Dad learned how to behave in different situations and in this one, that's what he felt he had to do to survive. The repercussions of his dalliance might have been worse had the townspeople and the school not had a vested monetary interest in him. Black people in the South were being hanged for less than what he was doing.

Unfortunately, Dad also experienced some issues while traveling with the team. When he led the University to the Hawaiian Classic, he got off the plane and watched as all the Hawaiian girls put leis around his teammate's heads and gave them a kiss on the cheek. When it was his turn, they put the lei around his neck, kissed their own hands, and then touched his cheek. Later that day, he told the coach he wasn't going to play the game because of what had happened. The coach immediately lined up all the Hawaiian girls and made each of them kiss him. This was an example of a stand for civil rights that went unnoticed by many.

Dad excelled on the basketball court. When he came to Portland, the entire sports program changed. He was Portland's "Handy" Andy Johnson, a moniker he was given because of the enormous size of his hands, which came in handy for ball-handling. Dad broke every basketball record including the high jump at the school and was later inducted into the University of Portland's Hall of Fame with statistics that in some cases have yet to be matched. In fact, while he was there, the university had the highest attendance at basketball games it's ever had—even to this day.

Dad was in the 1,000 Point Club and the 20 Rebound Club between 1950 and 1953, and he was the major driver in the drastic turnaround of the coaching record. Mush Torson, Portland's head coach from 1946 to 1954, became the third winningest coach in the school's history with 144 wins, most led by the scoring of Andy Johnson. All of the number one teams that defeated Portland in previous years were now decimated due to Dad's leadership. How ironic it is that Dad was an All-American—but in many ways didn't receive the respect and treatment the title implies.

Sadly, Dad seldom went to class, although he did attend his psychology class fairly regularly (where I think he picked up some of his matchless parenting philosophies). Although he admitted that the only reason he went to psych class was because the professor gave him money. Dad had finally fully realized Uncle Carl's lesson on the power of money.

"The only time I would see a teacher was at the games. They didn't care as long as I was putting the basketball in the hoop. "—Andy Johnson

The more he excelled in basketball, the more Dad was praised, and the more the school tinkered with his transcript. It was as though basketball became a career for him as soon as he started playing organized ball back at North Hollywood. Basketball was not the supplement to a good education, as it was for most of his teammates. Basketball was his educator. His coaches were his professors. The court was his classroom. He learned how to strategize, anticipate, rebound, defend, and score in everyday life because that would be the only way he'd learn. The system valued the growing attendance at games, increasing revenues, and publicity more than the reading and writing abilities of the one who made it all happen.

It might have been different if none of Portland's athletes had to attend classes; if it was an issue of special treatment for athletes in general and not a disregard for the education of one black athlete in particular. But that wasn't the case. Dad said that many of the guys on the team were angry with him because he didn't go to class while they had to—and if they did poorly in the classes that they *were* attending, they'd be kicked off the team. So, the school had a policy in place when it came to athletes and grades, it just seemed to forget about those policies when it came to their money-making forward, Andy Johnson.

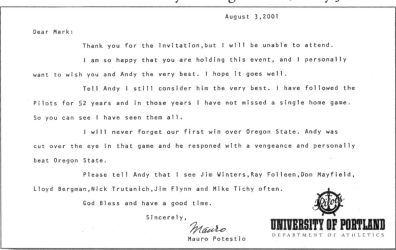

Letter from Mauro Potestio who never missed a Univeristy of Portland home game. Over the course of 857 games since 1950, no one in Pilots history has seen more games than Potestio, who recently was honored by Portland for his longtime support.

Forever embedded in my memory is the day in 2000 when Dad and I received a copy of his college transcript, which showed three years of classes and grades. His response was, "What class is that? I never took these classes!" Granted, it had been sixty years since he'd attended Portland so he could have forgotten about a professor here or a class there, but I doubt he'd forget all of them. Dad was adamant that he never went to or even registered for ninety percent of the classes on his transcript. Actually, if you look at a copy of the transcript, you can clearly see how the university kept him there by erasing grades and dropping courses with teachers that would not "play ball" and give him grades in exchange for no work.

I often wonder what would have happened had Andy Johnson stayed at Portland for four years. Would they have given him a degree? In what? When I researched the course descriptions for the Liberal Arts degree they had listed on his transcript, only some of the courses matched. In fact, I found if I followed the dates on his transcript and cross-referenced them with when Dad was breaking records for the school, I was able to see how they were keeping him in school for their own purposes—which explains why when Dad left for the Harlem Globetrotters, they didn't give him random grades as they had before. They flunked him out.

How ironic it is that years later, when Andy interviewed for a coaching position at the University of Portland, he was denied the job because he didn't have a college degree.

Note: It wasn't until ten years later, in the early 1960s, that the *Washington Post* reported that the University of Maryland decided to offer "Negroes" athletic scholarships. Although there was one stipulation: they had to meet academic requirements.

FFICIAL SOUVENIR PROGRAM

ABE SAPERSTEIN'S
FABULOUS

HARLEM
GLOBETROTTERS

basketball's
no. 1
show

33 rd season
1959-60

3

The Original Harlem Globetrotters

THE WAY DAD EXPLAINED IT, the Harlem Globetrotters were, above and beyond any other label, known as the "freaks of basketball." As they traveled the world in true ambassador fashion, audiences everywhere knew one thing for certain when the team stepped onto the court wearing its trademark red, white, and blue uniforms: these basketball magicians were going to entertain them more than they could ever imagine.

The Globetrotters' history is pivotal to understanding modern-day basketball. Mr. Naismith might have created the game but the Trotters took basketball further than it had ever been. Abraham Michael Saperstein, owner of the Trotters, took the game of entertaining basketball and ambassadorship globally. The team had guys that could do ridiculous and amazing things. In fact, in many ways, the Harlem Globetrotters was like a circus. Boid Buie, who had one arm, would place the basketball under the nub that jutted out from his shoulder and perform moves that many players with both arms could only dream of doing, including amazing dunks. He averaged eighteen points a game. Some say Leon Hilliard didn't have any arches in his feet, so when he dribbled you couldn't tell which direction he was going. And, we must remember one of the greatest Globetrotters of all time, Mr. Goose Tatum—a ringmaster on the court.

Some of the Trotters had arms so long they could stand flat-footed and reach up and touch the basket rim despite the fact that they were only six feet tall. And let's not forget the basketball circle, where the players performed a lot of tricks, all while that Sweet Georgia Brown music played.

Abe, as everybody called him, was born in the Irish-German White Chapel district of London on July 4, 1902. Around 1921, after emigrating to the States with his family from Poland to escape Russia's severe terrorization of the Jews, he played for a local amateur basketball team called the Chicago Reds. Four years later, he became the coach. At about this time, a star pitcher for the Negro Baseball League's Chicago American Giants, Walter Bell, called upon Abe to help coach his failing basketball team. Walter Bell also owned the all-black team in Chicago and was associated with the American Legion's Giles Post.

Harlem was in its heyday and on one of their trips there, Walter and Abe visited the Savoy Ballroom, a popular nightclub, where they connected with the Savoy Big Five basketball team. Ultimately, Abe ended up taking three of the players, Inman Jackson, Lester Johnson, and Walter Wright, to be pioneer members of what would soon become known as the Harlem Globetrotters.

Abe wanted to take the team global because he had a vision and knew the world was lacking in true sportsmanship. He also realized that most of the world had never seen black players with these skills before. Several historians and people close to the team have alleged that Abe actually co-owned the Globetrotters with the first black players but eventually took over the team when he grew tired of splitting the proceeds. .

"Everybody should have their passport. It gives you an opportunity and a chance to see farther than your own neighborhood."—Andy Johnson

Abe was known to seek out unique players. Dad would joke that Abe found him shooting peanuts in a Coke bottle which, while untrue, was not uncharacteristic of the lengths Saperstein would go to find players. Abe traveled across the country in search of the best black basketball players, finally assembling the Original Harlem Globetrotters in 1927, not in New York, but in Chicago, his hometown. In the early days, the Globetrotters were a barnstorming team, which simply meant that owners like Saperstein would form a team, go into Any town, USA, and play the best teams of that town, creating what are now known as exhibition games. Abe had a monopoly on nearly all of the phenomenal black players.

When you think about it, barnstorming wasn't much different than sharecropping. The "harvest" was the money generated from the games—the "crop"—and owners like Saperstein would pay the players a miniscule share of what the crop rendered, despite the fact that the harvest was the sole result of the players' hard work. These guys played 200 games a year, which sometimes meant two or three games a day, five to seven days a week. In fact, the Trotters once played four major games in one day. A record that still stands today.

Nonetheless, many teams who played against the Trotters didn't plan on the degree of their impending defeat. In fact, clowning around and the entertainment aspect became an integral part of the games as a result of the humiliating losses the home teams incurred when playing against the Trotters. These guys played so many games they had to figure out how to get rest and that is when they started the dribbling, baseball, and confetti-in-the-water-bucket gags. Saperstein observed the way the mind-blowing dunks, passes, and jump-shots turned on the crowd. To make a hook shot from half-court four out of five times, like Globetrotter star Bob "Showboat" Hall did—well, that was (and is) amazing!

As to the ubiquitous question of whether basketball players today are more skilled or more athletic than those of my dad's generation, my dad, of course, didn't think so and neither did any of his Trotter teammates that I spoke with. Objectively, I have to side with the Trotters. If you watch any of the old film footage of the Harlem Globetrotter, you will be amazed at the ball-handling skills those guys exhibited, not to mention the conditions in which they played. But the biggest difference of all, I think, is that they were magicians with the basketball. Famed sportswriter Frank Deford said it best during a documentary I once saw: "It was like watching Michael Jordon and Eddie Murphy all wrapped up in one." They had to be. They had to stand out because they were always the outsiders and they had to get the home crowds to love them, even though they were the supposed underdog.

And, you must realize that the Trotters were playing in the midst of a major civil rights movement in our country. They had to deal with racism before and after the games and sometimes during. In some arenas they had to play two games; one for the black fans and another one for the whites. And due to Jim Crow laws, blacks would have to sit on one side of the court and whites would sit on the other, or blacks would be assigned to the nosebleed section.

These players had to perform under stressful conditions. Abe was a firm believer in the fundamentals and the rules of the game of basketball. Players in Dad's era out-thought their opponents and, as a result, created plays used today, such as the pick and roll and the three-man weave. Red Auerbach won championship after championship for the Boston Celtics with the Harlem Globetrotter three-man weave.

There was no way anyone could score 40 or 50 points on a Trotter, especially if he was being guarded by someone like Carl Green (described as one of New York City's greatest high school players), who was so fast and could bend so low he would almost drag his hand on the ground. Opponents would dribble the ball right into Carl's hand—and off to the races the other way went Carl!

I often argue that the Trotters of the 1950s and 1960s played more intelligently than the players do today. For example, they took defense very seriously. Yes, Michael Jordan is a legend in his own right but the key, from a Trotter perspective, would be to keep the ball out of his hands. He can't hurt you if he doesn't have the ball.

In addition, the Trotters were not allowed to let anything stop them from playing. Abe ran a tight ship; no matter what happened to a player, the show had to go on. My dad played a whole season with a broken hand because if he didn't play, he would be sent home with no money. Once Dad said Abe called a time-out in the middle of a game to tell the players in the huddle that the crowd wasn't into it; they didn't appear to be excited. So, he called down to the end of the bench and told another team member to go onto the floor and hit seven shots in a row in the game. The player knew he had to perform, so he hit nine shots in a row. Abe called time-out again. Dad and his teammates thought Abe was going to tell the player that he did a great job, but that's not what happened. Abe calmly said, "Now that we've got the crowd back, let's start the show." The Trotters were shocked—they thought that was the show!

That's what Dad dealt with. He needed to put food on our table so he played through the pain, both psychological and physical. Money wasn't a guarantee back then. Today, an injured player will be put on the injured reserve list and still receive a paycheck. Should a player have to when injured? No, not necessarily. But the fact that today's athletes know they don't have to play hurt has the potential to feed complacency and make them a little less tough than the players of Dad's generation.

***

The Harlem Globetrotters was a group of phenomenal ballplayers who weren't able to play professional basketball in leagues like the NBA because of racial segregation. It was inevitable that they would come to Portland seeking another star player, Andy Johnson.

It wasn't a long courtship, nor are there any dramatic commentaries on how my dad began playing for the Trotters.

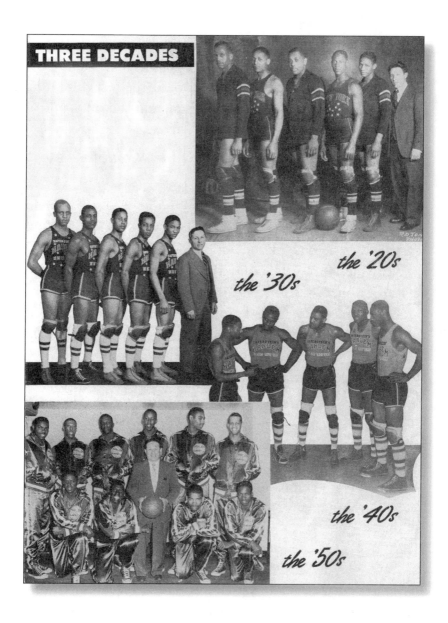

THREE DECADES

the '20s

the '30s

the '40s

the '50s

No, an unassuming black man showed up on campus, introduced himself as a scout for the Harlem Globetrotters, explained to my father how he'd noticed the recognition he was receiving as a college All-American, and laid out a pile of money on the bed.

"They sent a black man to fool me at college."—Andy Johnson

My father told me it was the most money he'd ever seen; in actuality it was seven hundred dollars in one dollar bills—an extremely generous amount of cash in 1953. Dad thought he'd hit the lottery! The only thing he had to do was sign a piece of paper and he could pocket the money. Instead of remembering Uncle Carl's lesson on the power of money, Dad only saw the opportunity to play for the team that he'd idolized as a kid. He viewed that chance as an honor and privilege—one that he wasn't going to pass up. My dad's response to the scout was typical Andy Johnson: "Not only will I sign that paper, but if you lean over far enough, I'll sign your forehead for all of that money."

Dad's journey as a Harlem Globetrotter—or at least his false start as one—began. It reminds me of when the slave trade started in Africa: their own countrymen led the new slaves right to the slave ships.

When Dad left the University of Portland, college officials were highly displeased. Their star basketball player, who never attended class and yet always earned grades for courses he never took, was leaving in his "junior" year to play for the Harlem Globetrotters. The university was not going to make that decision easy for Dad. Portland's disappointment at his choice to disrupt their winning streak and sign with the

Trotters was fully reflected in their alleged decision to contact the draft board of the United States Army. As a result, Andy Johnson took a slight detour from the Harlem Globetrotters and spent his first season in Fort Ord, a California barracks, playing for the Fort Ord Warriors.

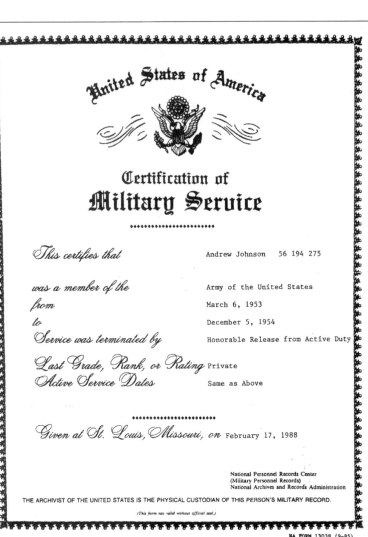

United States of America

Certification of
Military Service

This certifies that   Andrew Johnson   56 194 275

was a member of the   Army of the United States

from   March 6, 1953

to   December 5, 1954

Service was terminated by Honorable Release from Active Duty

Last Grade, Rank, or Rating Private

Active Service Dates   Same as Above

Given at St. Louis, Missouri, on February 17, 1988

National Personnel Records Center
(Military Personnel Records)
National Archives and Records Administration

THE ARCHIVIST OF THE UNITED STATES IS THE PHYSICAL CUSTODIAN OF THIS PERSON'S MILITARY RECORD.

(This form not valid without official seal.)

NA FORM 13038 (9-85)

4

Ball All That You Can Ball

D AD WAS HEADED BACK TO CALIFORNIA, although not to
North Hollywood. He was being sent to Fort Ord,
also known as "The Hill." Dad was one of many in
a diverse assembly of men slated to be trained for the Korean
War and any other Cold War activities of the U.S. Eligibility
applied to every male aged eighteen through thirty-five
regardless of race or occupation. Some had a military career in
mind while others were convicted felons who were given the
choice of jail time or the Army. However, for the most part,
Fort Ord, like many other military training facilities, housed
divorced men, non-critically disabled, high school and college
graduates, and dropouts. It was supposed to be an eight-week
basic training to become U.S. Army infantrymen. There were
few exemptions.

Top, left to right: "Detroit Bruce McLeod", boxing champion, Andy Johnson (University of Portland), Jerry (Diugy) Pease (USC), Bobby Pounds (UCLA). Bottom: Chuck Hollway, (UCLA football and track), Eru Bouyer.

Upon being drafted into the Army, Andy was placed in a special unit with other athletes, including boxers and football players. This wasn't unusual, except for the fact that they didn't have to deal with the fifty-five days of hell like everyone else. They didn't march in the bone-chilling fog or in the mud and rain. They didn't have to deal with grenades, bazookas, or tear gas. They didn't have guard duty—or any other extra duty. They didn't endure any of the strenuous rigors of post-basic training required of other soldiers. It must have felt like déjà vu to Dad, because while other soldiers were sweating it out and preparing to be sent to war, he and his athletic comrades were playing cards and pool. Not because they didn't want to serve their country, but because they were never asked to do anything more.

Andy knew he was in a special unit. While he may not have had to protect his country with machine guns and hand grenades, he served it and the other soldiers. Just like the famous and semi-famous folks before and after him, people like Elvis Presley, Andy Johnson wasn't required to do anything more than what he was born to do—play basketball.

"Even the army took me because I could play ball. They said I didn't have the I.Q. to actually be there."—Andy Johnson

As he would later do with the Harlem Globetrotters, Andy and his team brought people together for a brief respite during the war. Speaking of famous faces, Bruce McCleod, a friend of Dad's from the Army and a champion boxer, talked with me about the celebrities that bunked with them during their tenure in the Army. He vividly remembers sharing the barracks with top baseball player Billy Martin (Yankees and the Tigers), as well as other well-known athletes.

Andy played exhibition games with the Fort Ord Warriors, sometimes against the Original Harlem Globetrotters. Once again, he shot straight to the top as a standout on the team. Dad shared a story with me about the popularity of the Globetrotters and how everyone in his barracks claimed to play for them. Everyone would make up stories about playing with the Trotters, and you couldn't tell who was telling the truth and who was lying because there wasn't any television to confirm members of the actual team.

During this time, Abe Saperstein began putting together Globetrotter teams in other areas of the country. The Western Team, Southern Team, and short-lived Northern Team played the smaller towns and cities, just like in the early days, and the

Shooting For Title **Rainier Deal**

Fort Ord's Wonder Warriors

HERE IS the starting lineup that has carried the Fort Ord, Calif., basketball team into the Sixth Army finals at Fort Lewis. From left to right are Steve Pease (USC), Andy Johnson (Portland U), Bob Peterson (Oregon), Bobby Pound (UCLA) and Stan Albeck (Bradley). Inside the semi-circle is coach Glen Brown, formerly of Bradley.

Legendary coach Stan Albeck was a part of this team in his younger days.

Eastern Team, which consisted of the top talent, would travel to the larger venues, play the College All-Stars, and travel overseas. So it was possible that some of the guys played with the Harlem Globetrotters—but the truth is, they didn't. When the Harlem Globetrotters played an exhibition game at Fort Ord, all of the faux team members were exposed. The truth came to light that only Andy Johnson donned the star-spangled uniform and hit the court to the sounds of "Sweet Georgia Brown."

Unbeknownst to Dad at the time, he may have been "sold" again. Although never confirmed, it is suspected that the Globetrotters and the government cut a deal regarding my dad's status while in the Army. Dad received an honorable discharge after only a year and a half of active duty service, without one lick of actual service, which I still question.

There was a war going on. America was in the middle of a conflict between North and South Korea. Defending South Korea against a continuous barrage of artillery and a divided United Nations, the U.S. took a strong military stance against communism and those countries that supported it. We'd barely left Japan and the hostile battles of World War II when President Truman intervened.

Before long, basketball for Dad's service would not be enough. After a year and a half, Andy's unit was called to war. When Abe Saperstein heard that his star basketball player and ticket to franchise ownership was heading to war, he concocted another deal, this time in Dad's favor. He contacted one of the commanders at the base where Dad was stationed and allegedly exchanged Dad's honorable discharge for a benefit game held at the base. Thank God he did. I was told that shortly after Dad's unit was deployed, they were all killed in battle upon landing on foreign soil.

ABE SAPERSTEIN'S FABULOUS

Harlem Globetrotters

30TH SEASON

1956-57

IAL SOUVENIR PROGRAM

ANCHORAGE
HONG KONG
TOKYO
TAIPEH
GUAM
SINGAPORE
BANGKOK
DJAKARTA
HONOLULU
MONTREAL
SAN FRANCISCO
CHICAGO
NEW YORK
MEXICO CITY
PORT OF SPAIN
HAVANA
SAN JUAN
AUCKLAND
MELBOURNE
SAN SALVADOR
GUATEMALA CITY
PANAMA CANAL
BOGOTA
ASUNCION
LA PAZ
SANTIAGO
LIMA
CARACAS
EIRO
NTEVIDEO
TEL
ALEPPO
CAIR
BAGDAD
TUNIS
ALGIERS
BEYROUTH
TEHRAN
ISTANBUL
ATHENS
BELGRADE
MADRID
LISBON
ROME
VIENNA
BERLIN
PARIS
AMSTERDAM
GENEVA
LUXEMBOURG
BRUSSELS
LONDON
EDINBURGH
COPENHAGEN
STOCKHOLM

5

Finally, Trottin'

I N THE EARLY 1950s, young black boys didn't aspire to be NBA players, as they nearly unanimously do today. Instead, every black boy under the age of sixteen who loved basketball—from Montgomery, Alabama, to Chicago, Illinois, and from Brooklyn, New York, to Compton, California—wanted to be a Harlem Globetrotter. Overseas, the admiration was even more astronomical. A 1958 *Jet* magazine ad featured a young kid bouncing a ball around at three o'clock in the morning and when a man asked him what he was doing, he responded incredulously, "I'm practicing to be a Harlem Globetrotter."

Andy Johnson was no exception. As I said earlier, he first saw the Trotters play with Uncle Carl in the Pacific Arena in California during the late forties. It wouldn't be long before he'd get his chance to play in the same stadium.

Only legitimate talented athletes played for the Harlem Globetrotters. The team proved its talent publicly in 1948 when the Trotters beat the World Champion Minneapolis Lakers (now known as the Los Angeles Lakers) in an exhibition game. That game was important for two reasons: First is that it was a time of civil rights and democracy in America and that is how many people viewed this game against the all-white Lakers and the all-black Trotters. Secondly, this was to be Abe Saperstein's shot at getting an all-Negro franchise team into the NBA. However, not wanting to admit to the athletic prowess of the Trotters and because of the small margin by which the Trotters won, many NBA fans and the media chalked up the Trotters' win as luck. The following year, the Trotters had a rematch against the now two-time World Champion Lakers, only to beat them convincingly.

This defeat is a testament to the athletic prowess of the Harlem Globetrotters of the forties, fifties, and sixties. It wasn't just about clowning around on the court for these guys. Yes, they did entertain the crowds, but they were also ballers in every sense of the word. In contrast, could the Globetrotters of today beat the World Champion San Antonio Spurs? It's unlikely. The reality is that the Trotter talent is not at the level it was in Andy's era. This is because Abe no longer has a monopoly on all the great black ball players. The other reason is that the NBA is now

Andy Johnson, Harlem Globetrotter rookie.

allowing blacks into the league. So, essentially the NBA of today is the Harlem Globetrotters and the Harlem Ren's of yesteryear.

Despite beating the Lakers two years in a row, Abe did not get his team; however basketball was never the same after that and the

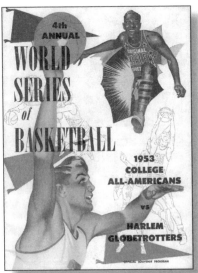

By 1963 crowds of almost 300,000 people would attend these series of games.

world took notice of the amazing talent on this black team called the Harlem Globetrotters. America wanted to see more of these guys on a consistent basis. And the only way that was going to happen was for the Trotters to transition into the NBA. Many people began to question why the Harlem Globetrotters weren't in the NBA.

The NBA also took notice and, at this point, started to evaluate their policy. African Americans were finally introduced into the NBA. Much like they do today, the NBA and the Trotters found their talent through the four-year colleges and universities. During the late forties and early fifties, and only slightly before the integration of the league, the Globetrotters became the measure of that talent. Abe Saperstein, marketing genius that he was, worked with the NBA in the coordination of the College All-Star team, a group of the top basketball players from colleges and universities across the country. This team would play against the Harlem Globetrotters in national exhibition tours across the country, games that would pack the stands and stadiums to capacity.

The College All-Star teams weren't slouches. As a matter of fact, the coaches' polls determined the teams, which consisted of some of the greatest NBA players of all time, men like Bob Cousy, Kevin Oshea, and Paul Arizin, who'd later play with Andy in Philadelphia with the NBA's Warriors team. The teams' top-notch coaches included Ray Meyer, Hank Iba, and Claire Bee.

But, true to form, the Trotters prevailed. On April 9, 1951, the Trotters beat the College All-Stars in front of a crowd of more than 30,000 captivated fans. These exhibition games were huge draws for both the All-Stars and the Trotters. And, on one of those tours, Andy was the second-leading scorer. He was viewed as unstoppable.

It is ironic that Andy's enormous but often overlooked talent actually became the barometer against which future NBA talent was measured. In what were commonly known as CAGE Shows, the Harlem Globetrotters continually beat the College All-Stars, filling seats across the country. Famed sports-writer Gene Kessler noted that "where the U.S. Olympic champions, considered the greatest amateur squad ever assembled, failed to attract more that 15,000 in a two-day tournament, the Harlem Globetrotters are expected to lure more than that in one night." In that same article, he wrote that that Bill Russell, one of the greatest players actually acknowledged, would never be an Andy Johnson. How about that?

I had the privilege of witnessing one of the last unaired interviews of Wilt Chamberlain, filmed a few months before his 1999 death. The NBA great and former Trotter said, "If you were a young black kid in the forties, you wanted to be Joe Louis or a Globetrotter. Once I recognized my talent, I always knew where I wanted to be."

According to Wilt, he turned down a check for $100,000 to play for the Magicians (a team formed by former Globetrotters Marques Haynes and Goose Tatum), to sign instead with Abe Saperstein and the Trotters. Rather pointedly, he said that

Wilt Chamberlain, Harlem Globetrotter rookie.

HARLEM GLOBETROTTERS
They got dressed wherever they could and acted like brothers—
such as Dad and Carl make funny gestures about Rookie Brown's hair.

Bottom row, left to right: Oliver "Catfish" Rollins, Clearance Wilson, Rookie Brown, Leon Hillard. Middle row: Woody Saulsbury, Earnest Wagner, Andy Johnson, Carl Green, Ben Jackson. Top: Meadowlark Lemon.

the NBA never gave him the fulfillment that being with the Globetrotters did.

"The fraternity of the Globetrotters was one of the most rewarding times of my life. I almost did not go into the NBA," Wilt stated. Many people don't realize that Wilt Chamberlain not only changed the game of basketball on the court but off the court as well. He opened the floodgates for minority ball

Newspaper caption reads: Globetrotters Beat the Minneapolis Lakers, 61-59, as Gun Sounds....

Winning basket in Air at Game's End; 17,853 Go Wild!! By Edgar C. Green

players to receive the big salaries that they command today. Wilt also demanded that the team owners not book games in towns where he could not eat after the games because of the Jim Crow laws. Many food establishments would claim that they were "practicing," which meant blacks were not allowed to eat in the restaurant.

Money was one thing but when it came to talent, Wilt felt as though it was a step down to play in the NBA.

```
3Jan58
Chicago, IL
```

Minneapolis Lakers	FGM	FTA	FTM	PF	PNTS
Vern Mikkelsen, F	1	7	6	5	8
Ed Fleming, F	4	10	7	5	15
Art Spoelstra, F	0	3	1	6	1
Dick Schnittker, F	3	3	3	1	9
Larry Foust, C	8	19	14	2	30
Jim Krebs, C	8	6	6	5	22
Dick Garmaker, G	2	5	2	3	6
Bob Leonard, G	6	0	0	2	12
Rod Hundley, G	3	1	1	2	7
Walter Devlin, G	0	1	1	1	1
Totals	35	55	41	32	111

Harlem Globetrotters	FGM	FTA	FTM	PF	PNTS
James	0	0	0	1	0
Andy Johnson, F-C	15	15	7	6	37
Honey Taylor, G	0	0	0	0	0
Thomas Spencer, F	2	0	0	6	4
Clarence Wilson, G	1	2	0	1	2
Tex Harrison, G	3	10	7	2	13
Williams	3	4	2	6	8
Roman Turmon, C	1	4	3	1	5
Charles Hoxie, G	6	8	5	5	17
Ermer Robinson, F	0	0	0	0	0
J.C. Gipson, C-F	6	8	2	5	14
Totals	37	51	26	33	100

Ever since the Trotters beat the Lakers two times in a row, Abe never wanted them to beat the NBA team again in hopes the NBA would him allow to form an all-black team. These games, along with the College All-Stars, ended when those hopes died.

Carl Green, who played with Dad on the Trotters in the 1950s, agrees. "The NBA experience couldn't compare with being with the Trotters. You have a bunch of black guys from different parts of the country and you are traveling around the world, testing each other personally and growing together." They even developed their own language for when other people were around on and off the court, including their opponents, which exemplifies the kinship they felt with one another. "We could have conversations around other people and they would not have a clue what we were talking about," Carl states.

Playing for the Harlem Globetrotters from 1954 to 1957, Dad saw the world. Andy Johnson (NBA) was part of what was arguably the best Globetrotter team, playing alongside stellar sportsmen such as Willie Gardner (NBA), Sweetwater Clifton (NBA), Woody Sauldsberry (NBA), Meadowlark Lemon, Leon Hillard, Clarence Wilson, and New York legends Charlie Hoxie (LIU All-American drafted by St. Louis Hawks in 1955) and Carl Green (who left Philadelphia Warrior camp). This team operated like a symphony on the court; they had a language of

To The Harlem Globetrotters: In appreciation of their record in entertaining the service men of America in foreign states/status.—Dwight Eisenhower

their own that could not be duplicated. Wilt says, "They [the Trotters] were the best at what they were doing."

The U.S. State Department under President Eisenhower named the Trotters "Ambassadors of Goodwill." In the early 1950s, they traveled to Europe, the Far East, Australia, South America, Mexico, and the Caribbean Islands. The Harlem Globetrotters

THE GLOBETROTTERS
VISIT
BOYS' TOWN OF ITALY

Russia

Alaska

Above: Walter Kenndey (Former president and commissioner of the NBA), Abe Saperstien (Trotters), Eddie Gotlieb (Warriors), and Nikita Khrushchev (led the Soviet Union during the Cold War). Trotters (T. Harrison and C. Wilson).

The Harlem Globetrotters were the first sports team to travel and show true ambassadorship by showing kids all over the world that they cared, from visiting orphanages in Italy to holding free basketball clinics in Slavic countries.

were the first to bring this style of basketball overseas. The world was their playground as the joy of the sport became kinetic and they transferred their energy into the hearts of their fans. They even taught basketball clinics in a number of different countries.

In those days, Abe not only took basketball around the world, he also brought the floor. Many of the venues the Trotters played at did not have a proper playing surface, so the hardwood floor traveled with the team. Before they started to bring flooring, they played on surfaces that you can't even imagine. In Germany, they played on broken beer barrels; in New Zealand, cow patches; in Italy, an ice rink covered with plywood; and in Spain, the bull ring—and it wasn't always cleaned after the last bull fight. Once they even played in an empty swimming pool, where one end was shallower than the other. And the Trotters continuously played in cold, rainy, and stormy conditions outside.

They even visited what was then simply a U.S. territory— Alaska. Playing in Alaska was a surreal experience, because instead of rowdy and loud cheers, the Trotters were met with complete silence by the Eskimos. The team later learned that in the Eskimo culture, the more silent the crowd, the more pleased and impressed they were with the team.

The Trotters packed venues from Wembley Arena in London to the Palais des Sport in Paris. In this aspect Dad got more education than he could ever have imagined as a boy growing up in North Hollywood—but the truth of the matter was that everything that glittered was not gold.

Some Trotters did not receive payment for the overseas trips because Abe convinced them that it was an all-expense paid trip to see the world. Of course, not all of the players bought into that lie. Dad was one of them.

Goose Tatum

And the exposure to these global experiences forced Dad to become more aware of the differences that existed in being a man of color. He began to question why the Globetrotters were treated better overseas than they were in the States.

The Trotters were the first Americans to be allowed behind what was known as the Iron Curtain (the Communist countries). The first Americans that many Russians saw was a group of black guys performing and showing true ambassadorship—while playing a lot of basketball. Abe and the Trotters gave the world the opportunity to see that these black men weren't defined by their race but were great human beings. They were always well-dressed and carried themselves in a respectable manner. Because of this, they were often asked to stay and live in the country in which they were visiting. Even though the Trotters never let on how they were segregated and treated back home, I believe some of the people in these countries knew of the struggles and obstacles that most blacks faced in the States. This was backed up by an October 3, 1960, article in the Chicago *Defender Newspaper* in which the leader of the Soviet Union, Nikita Khrushchev, spoke before the UN General Assembly on the mistreatment of Negros in the United States. Even with this knowledge, the Trotters were ambassadors of the United States and never let the fans from the other countries know how they were mistreated in their own country. Remember, this was when a strong civil rights movement was unfolding in the United States.

Andy Johnson and the other Trotters rarely feared for their lives when they were overseas. Most would venture into areas where they had been warned not to go. These guys, including Dad, wanted to meet the local people. Dad's saying was, "If you

Kutsher Country Club in Monticello, New York (left to right): Redd Fox, Helen Kutsher, Wilt Chamberlain, Milt Kutsher (owner of the famous Kutsher's Country Club where Wilt worked and played against other NBA greats), and Flip Wilson.

can walk among kings and queens and keep a common touch, then you have really made an achievement." Ernest Wagner, who also played with Dad, said, "I felt that they were using us for propaganda overseas. There was a heavy element of civil rights in the air. This was the time when the Emmett Till tragedy had taken place. They used us to down-play the seriousness of the civil rights movement."

Since rock-and-roll was still in its infancy, the Trotters were the rock stars of the era. As a result, the prejudices in America were painfully evident because of the glaring differences between their treatment overseas versus at home. Dad could walk down the Champs-Elysées in France in a suit and be treated like a celebrity. In America, he was adored on the court, but after the game, the he and the other team members couldn't find a restaurant to serve them dinner.

Dad usually used humor to sedate the anxiousness that inundated him as he and the Trotters approached a restaurant in some small town in the States looking for food. One evening, Dad and another teammate stepped into a small diner, where they encountered the abrasiveness of the owner, who said harshly, "I don't serve niggers!" Dad's teammate paused for a moment and then calmly said to the man, "Sir, I don't want a nigger. I want a cheeseburger."

This had been going on for a long time. Some of the earlier Rens recounted how they would have to stand in the kitchen to eat, so the patrons did not see them. Because of this injustice, the Trotters would buy food in a local market and make their own meals. They were resourceful in that way. Even in their sleeping arrangements, there were problems. Abe would stay in one hotel while the Trotters were forced to stay in a different one. At first, it was thought Abe did not want to stay with the team but it turns out that the team could not stay in Abe's hotel. I guess it worked out for Abe. He did not have to pay for the players to stay at a more expensive hotel. Sometimes they would have to sleep in private homes, two to a bed, because no hotel would accommodate them. Once they even had to sleep in a local jail.

Yet, in spite of it all, this Trotter team broke down many racial barriers. They often demanded their rights, both inside and outside the Trotter organization. This was proven during an interview with "Pop" Gates when he stated that in 1956, while he was coaching, he got word that the next scheduled game was in Birmingham, Alabama. They were on their way,

Sports programming featured the Globetrotters as the main basketball team. The 1955 team, which included dad, also hit the talk show circuit and appeared on very popular shows like The Ed Sullivan Show, The Steve Allen Show and the game show "What's My Line?".

when Pop phoned Abe to tell him that he did not think it was right to take the team to Birmingham with the rioting that was taking place. Abe ended up calling the game off, but Pop was taking a chance by standing up to Abe. Abe did not like anyone telling him how to run his plantation. People knew you had to be almost an "Uncle Tom" to stay around Abe. Realize, this was around the time Emmett Till was murdered. The team no longer wanted to play two games a night; one for blacks and one for whites. This was taking a toll on the players physically and emotionally. They eventually started canceling events until blacks and whites could attend the same game together. Segregation was still in effect, but changes were being made and the Trotters led that change.

A few oases existed for the players when they came home. In Harlem, the Trotters shared laughter, good times, and a brief respite in a black-owned establishment called Small's Paradise (Wilt eventually bought it and renamed it Big Wilt's Small's Paradise). The East Coast cities were jumping with clubs like Small's, where the spellbinding jazz, bebop, and soul music reflected the communities in which they thrived. Despite the turmoil that may have existed outside of this cocoon, the people—black people—had their own "Cheers," a place where everyone knew their name. After long, hard stints on the road, the Harlem Globetrotters relaxed in these places and many times they lent their presence to various spots in New York and Philadelphia, helping to build clientele, creating an audience, and validating rising comedians like Bill Cosby and Redd Foxx.

I used to wonder why Dad and the rest of the team didn't do more in the socio-political realm to force their better treatment outside of places like Harlem and Philly; now I realize they actually did more for civil rights than people imagine. There were times when a restaurant or a nightclub owner *would* bend the rules and allow the Globetrotters entry, and it was then that they showed these proprietors they were

The Globetrotters were used for everyday advertisement.

dignified and worthy of being there. This made it easier for the next person of color who tried to enter and ultimately, albeit slowly, broke down some of the walls of segregation that existed, if not physically, at least in the minds of some whites.

One way they did this was in the way they dressed. The Trotters were the first professional basketball team that wore suits before and after every game. (It's funny that today's pros were in such an uproar over the NBA's recent dress code enforcement.) When the team stepped out for a night on the town, whether they were in New York City, Tokyo, or Paris, these guys were always dressed to the nines and they teased the new guys on the team mercilessly until they finally brought themselves up to speed. The images of being impeccably dressed gentlemen made the fact that they were black go down easier for many who had a problem with that. Wilt recounts that Andy Johnson was "*GQ*" in the early 50s. He always wondered how Andy changed clothes two to three times a day while only traveling with two suitcases, one of which contained his uniform.

In addition to helping lessen the barriers of segregation, the Harlem Globetrotters brought joy and respite to war-torn countries and did their part to encourage peace in the post-World War II world and during the Korean War. In 1956, when the Trotters went to Lima, Peru, a civil war had broken out. Mass chaos spread, with shootings and fires exploding around the country. Amazingly, however, when the media found out the Trotters were about to arrive, each side called a four-day truce so the Trotters could keep their engagement. Needless to say, the fighting resumed after the Trotters left, but what an awesome impact this team had on the culture and the country. Gestures of this nature are probably why President Dwight Eisenhower took notice of the Harlem Globetrotters and deemed them ambassadors of the United States in the early 1950s.

The fact is, the Original Harlem Globetrotters introduced basketball to the world. Woody Sauldsberry, a former Trotter and 1957 NBA Rookie of the Year noted, "The only basketball that anyone overseas ever saw was from the Globetrotters. The NBA wants to take credit for that but they're just stealing the credit from where it's really due."

"Abe wanted it to be known that we'd transcended just being basketball players. We were human beings and representatives of our country," Wilt told a film crew in 1997.

While some people viewed Abe as a humanitarian, affectionately calling him Uncle Abe, there were many of Dad's colleagues who held another perspective of the little man with big ideas. Unfortunately, many of the players from the 1955-56 team roster did not hold Saperstein in such high regard when it came to the ownership and management of the team. Yes, the Trotters *were* known for inciting joy and excitement in their fans, but some serious internal struggles plagued the team as well.

Coach Gates often debated Abe about the fundamentals of the game and about wanting more money for the players. He knew Abe was getting rich while the players were killing themselves trying to earn a living for their families. Pop found out that the all-white traveling teams, along with the College All-Stars, were getting paid more money than the Trotters. He was very upset, so he decided to strike. He had one of the best teams ever assembled and knew that this new era of Trotters had the heart to stand up to Abe. It was perfect. They finally had Abe in a vulnerable situation. This attempt for equality quickly failed. Someone on the team told Abe about the plans for the strike. Immediately, Abe created several traveling Globetrotter teams that played simultaneously across the country. For this act of defiance, Abe dispersed the team that Pop felt could have excelled in the NBA, then and now. Abe was not quite done. The following season, Coach Gates received a telegram to report to the West team for the following year. Some players were sold off to the NBA while some, like Willie Gardner and my father, remained until the following season. Other players were forced into an early retirement.

According to Carl Green, who I spoke with at length regarding my dad's time with the Trotters, some critical cancers bubbled just below the surface of the happy faces the team donned on the court. "The Globetrotters had some very good players that were simply before their time. These were the older players from the forties, mostly from the South, who were more subservient and 'knew their place.'"

Abe and the coaches kept these players on the team because they helped keep the newer players in place. They essentially played one group against the other. "They [the older guys] would watch what we would say or do and report back to the coaches, all because we were a new generation of players that didn't bow to Abe," said Green.

Green stated that when he played, most of the players were from Los Angeles, New York, Philadelphia, and Detroit; whereas before, most of the players were from the South. It appears Saperstein exploited the natural differences in the mentality of these two groups of men to maintain the status quo of low pay and demanding schedules, as many team owners did. As much as he loved his father, Jerry Saperstein stated to me once in a rather matter-of-fact manner, "My father was a great visionary along with being a businessman, but not necessarily a good businessman."

By *good*, I believe Jerry meant *ethically*. There has never been a doubt that Abe was one of the team owners who maximized his profits by paying as little as possible to his players, in spite of the sometimes ridiculous conditions in which they had to work, travel, and stay. Abe treated his people like commodities and, in many ways, they were. Fairness wasn't an issue. This was proven in the earlier years of the Trotters. In 1939, a few of the players wanted a voice on how Abe ran the team because they did not think they were being treated fairly. Abe simply replaced the four players and kept moving right along. Goose Tatum and Marques Haynes left the Trotters in the early 1950s because of the unfair treatment. Abe was not concerned about being fair. He was concerned about making money.

People think when Nat "Sweetwater" Clifton went to the NBA, it was a great career move. Little do they know, Sweetwater left the Trotters because he and Abe did not get along. Abe told Sweetwater that he sold his contract to the NBA for five thousand dollars. He told Sweetwater that he would split the money with him; they were to each receive twenty-five hundred. Later, Sweetwater discovered that Abe actually cut a deal with the NBA for almost twenty thousand. Fairness was not in Abe's vocabulary. He tried to sell several of his players to the NBA. Abe did not care if players were hurt or tired. If he could book a game and get the money, he did it. The Harlem Globetrotters played more games than every NBA team did, combined, for an entire season.

"Abe treated you like you weren't there unless he needed you," says Green. "One time he came on the bus and gave Andy some money. Andy took the money but knew he wasn't going to play his 'game.' On the Trotters, you either had to be a good player or an Uncle Tom. I remember once when were on a European tour, I asked Abe for some more money. I was on the next plane home."

Green wasn't the only player who saw both faces of Abe and his player cronies. Woody Sauldsberry, Jr. also expressed his frustration with the owner. "I didn't particularly like him. He was a funny little man who knew nothing about basketball. When we traveled, he come up to me and says, 'Hey, Sauls, you're doing a great job,' and slip me five hundred dollars. I always thought that if we were getting paid what we were supposed to, he wouldn't have to do that."

But that was how Abe maintained control.

Abe even tested Dad on occasion. One time on a European tour, Abe threatened Andy by saying that all he knew was basketball and he wouldn't be able to do anything else with his life. In true Andy Johnson fashion, Dad came back with a quip that, ironically, Abe probably still remembers, even in the afterlife. Andy said, "I will go back home and be a gravedigger, Abe, and I will definitely keep in touch."

"I left school and went with the Harlem Globetrotters not knowing that, one more time, I would find myself being used like a rag and there was nothing that I could do about it."—Andy Johnson

Despite the drama, one thing was a constant in the Trotters' camp during my dad's time with the team: the respect and admiration that many of the players had for Andy. Initially I was only aware of Dad's influence on the Trotters, through his own stories and the conversations I had with his friends and fellow teammates, like Carl Green, Charlie Hoxie, and Woody Sauldsberry; however, Wilt Chamberlain solidified and confirmed Dad's impact in his 1997 interview when he gave the ultimate accolade about Dad: "I had the pleasure to first see Andy Johnson playing with the Globetrotters in Philadelphia, and he was a great shooter. As a basketball player, of course you loved the humor of the game, but you also looked for the Trotter who had the real skills. Andy Johnson was one of those who could really play the game. Several years later, I got a chance to meet him personally, when I joined Andy and the Philadelphia Warriors. Andy Johnson became my mentor."

Woody also said, "Andy was a great player. You could say a superstar. He had a killer instinct."

The Globetrotters set the standard when it came to the true essence of basketball, having some of the strongest and most talented players in the world. And, as with most American enterprises, the NBA found a way to capitalize on that. Some of the first blacks to join the NBA were Harlem Globetrotters. In 1958, they found their way to Andy Johnson.

One of my father's favorite modeling pictures of my mom. (Barbara Billingslea-Johnson)

6

Love at First Sight

TWO THINGS THAT STOOD OUT about Andy Johnson were his strength and his self-confidence. He had a commanding presence. A final growth spurt landed him at six feet, five inches and 225 pounds. More than being a big man, Andy was solid and had nearly zero percent body fat. With his brawn, many people described his build as being like that of a heavyweight prizefighter.

It is ironic Dad was compared to a boxer because, during my research, I found that Dad actually had an amateur boxing career. The driving force behind it, as short-lived as it was, was one of the premier fight manager/promoters of the day, Sid Flaherty. Sid ran a boxing gym in San Diego and was well-known because of fighters such as Carl "Bobo" Olsen, the 1953

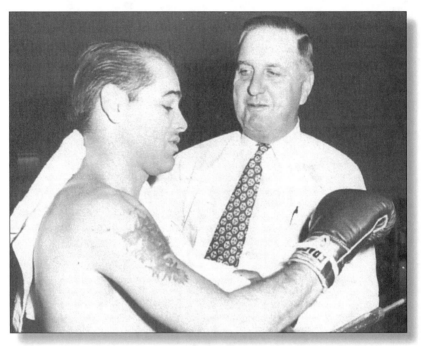

Sid Flaherty (manager/promoter) with Carl "Bobo" Olsen, 1953 Middleweight Champion.

Middleweight Champion. (Bobo beat England's champ Randy Turpin in a fifteen-round battle for the title that Sugar Ray Robinson abandoned.) Sid would pull fighters from Hawaii to Mexico and was known for promoting the entire card for the Bill Miller Shows at the Famous Silver Slipper in Las Vegas. Sid wanted Dad to be one of his fighters really badly.

It's not as uncommon as one might think to see athletes dabbling in more than one sport, particularly during a time when athletes were not getting paid the millions of dollars that they do now. The great Bob Gibson, the St. Louis Cardinals' World Series pitching hero, toured with the Trotters; and famed Trotters Goose Tatum and Meadowlark Lemon were actually baseball players. So, while basketball was Dad's first love, he was definitely open to other opportunities in sports. As a matter of fact, the revered jazz and pop singer Frank Sinatra supposedly offered Dad $50,000 to box. With an amateur record of 35 wins out of 37 fights, his success was quite possible.

When I was told about Dad's boxing matches, I wondered what would have happened if he had decided to pursue boxing as a career instead of basketball. Could he have given a young Cassius Clay a run for his money? Or would he have ended up like many fighters of that time, whose prowess made tons of money for their promoters and very little for themselves? I guess it's irrelevant considering that Andy bled rubber. Basketball was his heart.

I'm not sure if it was his size that gave Dad the confidence he exuded; all I know is that until he died, he had it. With a silent strength and poise, Dad exemplified the ability to "walk amongst the common man with a king's touch." He garnered this ability from firsthand experience as he met kings, queens, princes and princesses, diplomats, and top political figures. He learned from the best on how to carry himself and that sense of self came across in everything he did and everything he said. This would be most evident in my Mom and Dad's first meeting at the club inside the Evans Hotel.

Dad had access to women from Philly to Mozambique. He carried himself like most of the guys during this era, with hair conked (peroxide in the hair to make it straight) and slicked, all to impress the women they came across. They would say that their hair was fried, dyed, and laid to the side.

As an athlete, Dad was a rock star in every sense of the word. When Wilt Chamberlain stated in a book that he'd slept with a lot of women, the world was in an uproar. Dad wasn't. They

"When I was young and dumb and full of come... I had too many girls to choose from. Now I am old and ready to fold... Any one girl is worth a pot of gold."—Wilt Chamberlain

traveled the world and many times women, multiple women, came with the territory. Dad had been around the world and had met the most fascinating women. But he felt that all those women could not compare to the love he had for his wife . . .

Mom was on a date—*with someone else*. Dad saw her, and despite the fact that Dad was a recognizable sports figure and women were constantly throwing themselves at him, he was determined to have this particular woman. He told me that she was like a princess, the most beautiful woman he'd ever seen. That's not hard for me to believe, not because she is my mother, but because mom was a model. She was a *JET* and *Sepia* (compared to *Ebony*) magazine model. These magazines were one of the first publications to feature news and entertainment related to the black community. While most magazine covers in the fifties featured white actresses like Rita Hayworth, Mitzi Gaynor, Jean Simmons,

Barbara Billingslea-Johnson.

and of course, Marilyn Monroe, a *JET* model was the epitome of black beauty to most men. (Today, men still look at the center of *JET* magazine for the *JET* Beauty of the Week.)

So, being the proud and self-assured man that he was, Dad walked over to the table and sat down. Yes, Dad sat down in the chair next to Mom and her date and began talking to her. In fact, Dad turned to the guy and explained to him that he would like to take a moment and speak with the young lady. Needless to say, Mom's date was so stunned, and possibly embarrassed, by the large basketball player who'd all but stolen the attention of his girl, that he stood up and left the table.

And, that was the beginning of Andy Johnson and Barbara Billingslea's love affair. Dad desperately wanted to marry her, but on the salary that he was making, he didn't have enough money to buy a ring. However, six months after Dad's charismatic approach in the Evans lounge, on November 15, 1957, Mom and Dad were married.

It was true love at first sight.

"It might not be you she likes. It just might be the uniform."—Andy Johnson

My mother was a special lady. I believe she was what the old folks call "before her time." She was a beautiful woman who cooked and cleaned and raised her kids. She was the type of mother who had me attending the school of the performing arts while my sister, Ann, by the age of thirteen, was dancing with one of the top dance companies in Philadelphia. She steered my brother, Andrew Jr., right to college on a football scholarship.

This was Dad's first and only marriage but Mom's second of three. My mother had been previously married and had three small children from that union. Not only did my father gain a wife, but he also acquired a ready-made family that he accepted, supported, and cherished. My parents had three children together, of which I am the youngest.

My mother was the love of Dad's life, despite the fact that they separated when I was in the eleventh grade. In spite of the separation, a love and connection existed between them that was undeniable, along with a friendship that would carry their relationship well past their divorce. But life got in the way, as it often does, and if you don't know how to hang on, sometimes it's easier to let go.

Carl Green knew them both: "Andy lived in a world that if you were a dark-skinned black man and didn't take no mess, you didn't get anything handed to you. If you were light-skinned or subservient, you could be set up as an example for other blacks. After basketball, when Andy worked in the prison, Barbara wanted more. She came from a different life. She couldn't fully understand his world. They just came from two different worlds and that got the best of them."

Knowing that he would already be stereotyped because of his dark skin, Dad refused to take any mess, as he would call it, from anyone. The kind of prejudice that comes from within your own race, the whole notion of a person being better or even more attractive if they were lighter, was foreign to him. Yet he began to come across some lighter-skinned black people who felt as though they were better than their darker-skinned counterparts. There were those who found it unbelievable when they'd see a tall, dark, and handsome man like Dad leave a game with a fair-skinned beautiful lady. Mom was different, though. She didn't see things in those terms, even if people outside of their relationship did.

Much of the downfall of my parents' marriage was financial. Mom was frustrated by how much the white players on the Warriors were being paid

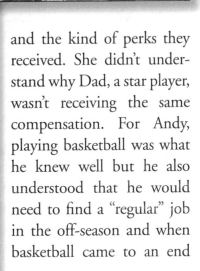

and the kind of perks they received. She didn't understand why Dad, a star player, wasn't receiving the same compensation. For Andy, playing basketball was what he knew well but he also understood that he would need to find a "regular" job in the off-season and when basketball came to an end for him. He was keenly aware that, unlike today, there wouldn't be any large endorsement contracts or opportunities to open businesses. I'm sure Mom was frustrated by that, especially after all of the sacrifices they had made.

Once Mom, being the colorful person that she was, walked into the office of the Philadelphia Warriors' owner, Eddie Gottlieb, and holding Dad's check in her hand, told him that they could not live off the amount of money they were given. She then proceeded to turn the water cooler over onto his desk. Although that wouldn't have been his approach, Dad backed her up because he knew she was right and she was fighting for her family. However, eventually that ran thin for the both of them. At the time of their separation, I didn't understand what irreconcilable differences meant, but later I learned first-hand what my mother and father went through as I struggled through my own divorce.

Another issue that impacted my parents' relationship was how Dad viewed Mom's level of support while dealing with his troubles with his career. Dad grew up watching Aunt Mildred deal with Uncle Carl's alcoholism with grace, understanding, and patience. When Uncle Carl came in from work and passed out on the floor, she'd simply pull him to the shower, bathe him, and put him to bed. The next day she'd do it again. I think, in a way, Dad expected his wife to be that unconditional support system, without really thinking about her boundaries and where she might draw the line. Dad said he remembered going onto the court sometimes, after a heated argument with my mother, and not even realizing he was playing until halfway through the game. As a result, he stressed about her stress, which inevitably stressed the entire relationship to its breaking point.

The one thing I am proud to say is that whenever there was an issue with us kids, if one of us was sick or acting out, Mom and Dad always worked together in raising us. There were many times you wouldn't even know that they were separated. They didn't just talk to us, they talked to each other and in doing so, they found a way to raise their children without being married.

After they divorced, my dad had other relationships and my mom remarried. I think Mom remarried for companionship more than anything else and maybe because she was actively involved in the church she didn't want to carry on a relationship outside of marriage. Dad, on the other hand, had girlfriends, but often shared with me that no one would ever compare to Mom, especially since she was the mother of his most prized accomplishments—his children. In confidence, and despite having married again, my mother told me before she passed on Christmas Eve of 2000 that she never loved anyone like my dad.

I was in New York when my mother passed and I remember calling Dad, who was living in Allentown, Pennsylvania. Without hesitation, he met me in Philadelphia, at the hospital, along with my brother and sister, and I'll never forget what he did. As we viewed Mom lying peacefully on the bed, looking as though she was just taking a long, restful sleep, Dad bent his large frame over the bed and sweetly kissed her good-bye. Yes, despite it all, they really loved each other.

They made numerous trips to play in Hawaii. One of the teams they would play was the
Honolulu Surfrides

7

On the Road...Again

ONE REASON MY PARENTS' LOVE AFFAIR was so strong is because of the simple realities of the day. There were no cell phones, pagers, or email to keep in touch with loved ones while on the road; in those days, it was rough for many of the guys traveling. Nine times out of ten, they traveled by bus when they played in the U.S.

And, according to my dad, when they did fly, it wasn't the greatest experience in the world. In fact, after my father left basketball for good, he chose not to fly anymore. I remember asking him, "Dad, you've been around the world. Why don't you like to fly?" That's when he explained to me that when he flew with the Globetrotters he'd had the worst experiences you could have on a plane. "Planes weren't built like they are today," he'd say. The type of turbulence he described made it sound

OFFICIAL SOUVENIR PROGRAM

BASKETBALL'S NUMBER 1 SHOW

ABE SAPERSTEIN'S FABULOUS *Harlem Globetrotters*

28th SEASON

more like an SUV with wings instead of a jet. (Remember, the first passenger plane service did not occur until 1958 in a trip from New York to Miami.) Many of the planes that the Trotters traveled in did not even have seats; they were like cargo. And when they flew in military transport planes, the team had to wear parachutes. No, air travel was not like it is today.

Dad shared many stories about the in-flight adventures that he'd experienced as the Trotters roamed from city to city; from engines catching on fire after playing a game in Berlin's Olympic Stadium to finding out mid-air on a European tour that the plane was overweight and could not clear the mountains. In that incident, Trotters found themselves throwing out some of the luggage in order to lessen the weight load of the aircraft. Thank God that worked out!

Actually, one of the last times Dad flew, in the early fifties, started out the same as all the others: They lifted off the ground and the pilot made his usual announcements about the flight. However, twenty minutes later, Dad saw the pilot walk through the airplane rather quickly—not unusual, except that he had a parachute on his back. On this particular flight, none of the players wore parachutes, so you can imagine the expressions on their faces. Yet, Dad, being the silver-lining kind of guy that he was, covered his fear with jokes and laughter. He concocted a fake plot with other members of his team about how to get the parachute from the pilot if he dared to walk past them again.

Nonetheless, the awareness of his situation and his positive attitude are what kept my dad, and ultimately, his relationship with my mom, strong for a little while. He had to be mentally strong when he was on the road simply because he couldn't have regular contact with his family. Both Mom and Dad had to have a level of trust and understanding that most relationships couldn't withstand because it might be several days or a week before we'd hear from him, especially when he was overseas.

The guys on the road always gave each other a hard time. As I said before, this was a way to conceal the range of emotions they were feeling. One of the ways they would do this is by planting seeds of doubt about the fidelity of the wives and girl-friends back home. For instance, Dad would tell me that they'd be on a long bus ride, fourteen or fifteen guys, traveling on desolate Kansas roads, in the middle of nowhere, and in the midst of the silence, one guy would loudly begin to sing, off-key, a popular song by Jimmie Davis, "I wonder who's kissing her now."

Of course everyone would laugh, but inevitably the guys would begin to wonder about their relationships and whether their wives and girlfriends were at home or out gallivanting with some other guy. To find out, the guys, in true male fashion, would then make a bet. The next time they came to a telephone pole, which is where the antiquated phones were located on the side of the road, they would all phone home. Dad said that while waiting in line to use the phone, you could hear various teammates pleading aloud that their wife would answer so they would be able to withstand the teasing of the other players.

These pranks and jokes kept the morale up for my dad and his teammates. Besides not having the communication devices that we have today, they also didn't have portable music players. All they had was each other and they forged powerful relationships because of it. These friendships would supplement and support them through the very real problems that awaited them back home.

I think one of the things that helped my father, or at least offered perspective to him in getting through the problems that began to surface in his relationship with my mother, was the plight of one particular Harlem Globetrotter. While some of the Trotters would hang out at a bar and use their per diem to enjoy a few drinks, this man would save all of his money and send it back home to his wife. He was one of the first guys who'd wear a suit and tie all the time instead of just on the mandatory game days. He loved his wife almost obsessively. Yes, I know Dad loved my mother greatly, but Dad would always say that this guy talked incessantly about how much he loved this woman and would retell the story of their courtship any chance he got. He was consumed by her and would never do anything for himself. My dad and the other guys on the team would joke around with him, saying that it seemed as though he would not and could not exist without this woman in his life. They didn't realize how close they were to being right.

One time, the team went home for a stretch of time and when they returned, this teammate seemed extremely upset. Apparently, when he went home, he found that his suits had been tailored a little short. The team didn't think anything of it and they continued on with their season. Finally, they went home again and this time, upon returning for the next season, the guys found that this guy did not come back, which was not exactly unusual for the Globetrotter's ever-turning revolving door.

After skipping a season, the man returned, though not as a player but as one of the coaches. Dad and the rest of the team soon realized that something was different about him. He was agitated all of the time and as he was coaching, he began flipping out on the players. Dad said that being around him back then was like walking on eggshells. He had a short fuse, a temper that was on high alert. It wasn't until later that the guys found out that the man's wife, the woman he worshiped and adored, had split. They also learned that the reason he'd gone home that previous season and found his suits tailored differently was because his wife, the woman that he sent every dime to and loved almost to the point of obsession, was having an affair. She'd even gone as far as to tailor his suits to fit her new man.

After that one season of coaching, Dad said that no one ever heard from him, and they figured he'd simply taken time off to get himself together and then decided not to return to basketball. It wasn't until five or six years later that they'd get the heartbreaking ending to the story.

I remember Dad clearly saying to me as he told the story, "Mark, think of the worst bum that you have ever seen in your life. Now, think of the smelliest bum. Put them together and multiply it by ten. That image was this guy that was trying to get on our bus in this small town." Dad went on to tell me that the bus driver was trying to close the door, screaming at the guy to get off the bus, but Meadowlark Lemon said to let the guy on. Meadowlark asked the guys on the bus if they knew who the bum was and they said that they didn't. To the shock of everyone, Meadowlark announced that this smelly bum was the same man who'd played with them a few years back. My dad was stunned into silence. There were no jokes or pranks to explain away the pain of seeing a friend, a fellow Trotter, in that situation. Finally, they let him on the bus and gave him some food and money. Eventually they had to send him on his way, though and they never saw him again.

To my dad, it seemed as though this man had lost his mind over his wife's affair and it sent him into a tailspin of despair. I think my father learned that you can love somebody with all of your heart, but you don't want to be so consumed by the person that you'd lose your life if they should ever leave. This would prove to be prophetic later on.

I don't want to make it seem like all of the Trotters were not fully educated and had bad marriages. This is absolutely not the case. Many went on to be very successful in life.

Charlie Hoxsie, the 1957 MVP of the College All-Star tour, known as one of New York's finest ball players and an outstanding original Trotter, was an avid reader and known for his intelligence and education. And as far as relationships, there was no better marriage than that of my Uncle Carl Green

TROTTERS BEAT 49ERS—Andy Johnson of the Harlem Globe Trotters was surrounded by three San Francisco 49er ends when this picture was taken before a big crowd at the San Francisco Cow Palace last night. Left is Billy Wilson. No. 88 is Clyde Conner and right Forty-Niners gave a quarter but the stars won, 56 to Kalamazoo Monda 24th annual Milk

HARLEM GLOBETROTTERS
Ready to Play

Left to right: Ernest Wagner, Meadowlark Lemon, Leon Hillard, Woody Saulsbury, Carl Green, Oliver "Catfish" Rollins, Andy Johnson, Rookie Brown.

**ALLEY-OOP
IN REVERSE?**
*Andy breaks up an
alley-oop and turns
it into a field goal.*

GAME TIME

*Top row: Catfish Rollins, Carl Green, Andy Johnson, Ben Jackson, Woody Saulsbury, Rookie
Brown. Bottom row: Clearence Wilson, Meadowlark Lemon, Abe Saperstein, Ernest Wagner,
Leon Hillard.*

and his wife, Aunt Dean. As a young man, I would envision my wife being very much like her. I thought, and still believe, that the way they took care of each other was how a marriage was supposed to be.

But unfortunately, given the era, there were many Trotters during and before Andy's term with the team whose stories were similar to this man's—Trotters who ended up working as gas station attendants or other menial jobs and whose relationships and marriages were often broken as a result of the frustrations of their situations. Their personal lives were totally disconnected from the one they lived while traveling the world as "ambassadors."

And, the most disturbing reality is that, for the most part, we don't know these men's names. We learn of their contributions in passing and as happenstance, like when I found out that Zack Clayton (also a baseball player in the Negro League and first black man to referee a world title fight (Walcott-Charles IV in 1952), and the referee for the infamous and classic Muhammad Ali vs. George Foreman boxing match, was an original Harlem Globetrotter. It's interesting to me that these trailblazers played basketball for the love of the game—without any guarantees of security, financial or otherwise, and yet our Halls of Fame and sports industry celebrations often fail to mention their names.

PHILADELPHIA WARRIORS
vs
BOSTON CELTICS

ST. LOUIS HAWKS
vs
DETROIT PISTONS

Thursday, December 11, 1958
Convention Hall
Philadelphia, Penna.

25¢

Warriors Buy Andy Johnson From Trotters

New Player to Report For Hershey Drills

The Warriors have added a new player to their roster—6-6 Andy Johnson.

Owner Eddie Gottlieb announced the purchase of Johnson from the Harlem Globetrotters for a "substantial amount of money." Several other teams have been dickering for Johnson.

Johnson is not a stranger to them, since many of them played against him, either as College All-Americans on the annual Harlem Globetrotters' tour or in several exhibitions the Warriors have played with the Trotters.

Gottlieb said he hopes Johnson can make the transition to the National Basketball Association as well as another ex-Globetrotter, Woody Saulds-berry, did last season. Unheralded at the start of the season, Sauldsberry played so well he was voted the rookie of the year.

"We think Johnson will help us up front," Gottlieb said. "In his four years with the Globetrotters, he has proved his ability to shoot and rebound well enough to play in the NBA."

Last season the Trotters played the Minneapolis Lakers in an exhibition game and Johnson tallied 36 points. On the tours against the College All-Americans, Johnson always scored heavily.

Johnson played collegiate ball at Portland University.

8

Sold to the Warriors

IN THE EARLY NINETEENTH CENTURY, the primary source of income for America's citizens came from the selling and loaning out of slaves. As stated in *Chronology on the History of Slavery,* compiled by Eddie Becker in 1999, it was not uncommon to see signs posted saying "Cash for Negroes." Some 125 years later, not much had changed—only the wording.

To understand what was happening in professional basketball when my dad became a member of the Philadelphia Warriors, it is important to go back a bit and take a quick history lesson. The Philadelphia Warriors was part of the first basketball league, the American Basketball League (ABL). Started in 1925, the teams in the ABL were made up of mostly first-generation immigrants of Italian, Polish, Irish, and Eastern

European descent. The majority of these teams were Jewish and a fair share of prejudice existed even before blacks were allowed into the ABL.

Since blacks weren't able to fully participate in the ABL, the Harlem Rens were allowed to play in the ABL champion but not in the ABL World Championship and, as mentioned earlier, the Trotters played exhibition games. These two black teams, however, would barnstorm constantly, playing wherever they could and even meeting head-to-head on a couple of occasions.

One of the oldest teams out of Philadelphia was led by basketball mogul Eddie Gottlieb. He was associated with the Philadelphia SPHA (South Philadelphia Hebrew Association), formed in 1918. The championship team, made up of young boys from the American Jewish Club in South Philly, lasted for many years. The league survived until the Great Depression hit in the early thirties.

In 1937, the National Basketball League (NBL) resurfaced. This league was first established in the late 1800s. Companies like General Electric, Firestone, and Goodyear sponsored these teams, which were made up of mostly factory workers, most notably the great George Mikan of the Minneapolis Lakers. For the next several years, many teams would join the NBL and then later leave for a number of reasons.

Bill Jones in 1941 was the first to play on a integrated team with Toledo. Some other first were William "Pop" Gates of the Tri-City Blackhawks (now the Atlanta Hawks) and William "Dolly" King of the Rochester Royals (now the Sacramento Kings). Following their entry was Frank Washington of the Washington Bears, and Bill Farrow of the Youngstown Bears. These men were the first blacks to play professional basketball in a national league that would later become what we now know as the NBA; all four were products of the Rens or the Trotters. These four blacks had it pretty rough playing amongst the white players. The game got very physical at times for these players. One night Pop Gates got into a bad altercation with Chick Meehan of the Syracuse Nationals. The National Guard was called to calm fighting. The following year, all blacks were out of the league.

On December 17, 1947 the NBL invited the Harlem Renaissance to take over the franchise from the Detroit Vagabond Kings, which had folded midway through the season. They changed their name to the Dayton Renaissance and were the first and only all-black team to play in an all-white league. I don't know if the owners rushed to take advantage to get a team in the league. But, the Dayton Ren's was short lived. "Pop" stated that they were not getting paid. The team did not return for the following season. This was ultimately the end of the Harlem/Dayton Renaissance.

After World War II, arena owners in large cities were fascinated by how professional basketball could pack their houses. Arena owners Walter Brown (Boston Garden), Ned Irish (Madison Square Garden), and Maurice Podoloff (New Haven) retained ownership of the teams.

It was at this time when another basketball league was born—the Basketball Association of America (BAA) and when Eddie Gottlieb came back into the picture. Eddie co-owned the Philadelphia Warriors, along with his old friend Abe Saperstein, owner of the Harlem Globetrotters. This relationship would flourish with impeccable timing as the walls of segregation slowly began to fall in the professional leagues.

Big Doubleheader
HARLEM GLOBETROTTERS

BASKET BALL

In Person

HARLEM GLOBE TROTTERS

Featuring Philadelphia's own
Wilt (The Stilt) Chamberlain

Also
WARRIORS
vs
ST. LOUIS HAWKS
TAP-OFF TIME 8:00 P.M.
Convention Hall
Saturday December 27,

Reserved Seats $3.00, $2.50, $2.00, $1.50

Send checks to Warriors office
Sheraton Hotel, Philadelphia

Andy fights for the ball.

PHILADELPHIA VS. BOSTON
Bill Russell grabs a rebound as Andy Johnson and Wilt Chamberlain look on.

94

In 1949, these two rival leagues, the NBL and the newly formed BAA, merged into the National Basketball Association (NBA). In the transition, one thing was lost: the ability for blacks to play in the league.

But the all-white NBA didn't last for long. In the midst of the deal-making, the league couldn't afford any negative press and there were no competitive reasons why blacks couldn't play the sport with whites, especially since the Harlem Globetrotters had beaten the World Champion Minneapolis Lakers twice. In addition, the all-white teams were not drawing the crowds. In fact, Harvey Frommer, a sportswriter at Dartmouth University, describes one of the earlier segregated NBA games as being "a yawner of all yawners."

Enter Abe Saperstein with the hottest team in the country—the Harlem Globetrotters—that drew record crowds whether it was playing the College All-Stars repeatedly, garnering an attendance of almost 200,000 people, or making its mark and filling stadiums all over the world. The NBA wanted a piece. They were losing money and losing it fast. The NBA started with seventeen teams in the league and ended that first year with eleven. People wanted to see the flying dunks of the all-black Trotters; so Eddie Gottlieb, a major player in the NBA by this time, called up his good friend Abe Saperstein and made a deal.

They were both involved in scheduling for the two organizations, and Saperstein came up with the concept of hosting exhibition games between the Harlem Globetrotters and NBA teams. As mentioned before, few people attended the NBA games until the Trotters began playing them in exhibitions. Gottlieb and Saperstein capitalized on the fact that people wanted to see the type of basketball that the Trotters exhibited, and the doubleheader was born. Wherever the NBA played, Saperstein would bring the Trotters in to play the first game. So, while it is doubtful that it will ever go out in a press release, the Harlem Globetrotters were responsible for not only catapulting the NBA into its success in the 1950s but also in making sure that the league did not fold.

Technically, Abe was the first agent to the NBA. He had been recruiting and signing all the talented black players and putting them under his contract for years; he had the monopoly on them. Some of the Trotters would get invited and drafted to the NBA tryout camps but would be released because Abe and the NBA could not agree on the money. Inevitably the NBA began to consider bringing on black players directly and skipping Abe as the middleman. They thought they could garner success like Saperstein's by allowing a few black players onto their teams as tokens. But this type of success would not be immediate; remember, Abe had a thirty-year start on recruiting these phenomenal players—and not all of the NBA teams were anxious to get their first black player.

In 2002, Marc Spears wrote an article on ESPN.com in which current Globetrotter owner Mannie Jackson said, "The Harlem Globetrotters beat the so-called champion Minneapolis Lakers two years in a row [referring to the Trotters' 1948 and 1949 wins over the then NBA champs] ... integration [into the NBA] was accelerated because it was realized that the best basketball players weren't in the NBA." He forgot to mention that the NBA also wanted to fill all those empty stadium seats.

Considering that the average playing time of a Harlem Globetrotter was only three to four years, due to the grueling travel schedule, the NBA posed a financial and physical benefit to the Trotters who were able or wanted to make the transition.

ANDY JOHNSON   Phila. WARRIORS   No. 12   Ht. 6'6''   Wt. 220   Portland

Viewing the demographic makeup of the NBA today, it is hard to believe that quotas ever existed. But they did. In the 1950s and 60s, the NBA was letting black players in—in Noah-like fashion, two by two. This meant that each team in the NBA had an unwritten rule that gave a maximum quota of two black players per team. Since there were eight teams in the NBA at the time, only sixteen black players could actually be signed at any given moment. And all sixteen were never drafted at once. It was usually on a one-here, one-there basis.

All eight teams followed the rule to draft players of color. There was just one problem: not all of the organizations kept the black players they drafted. This is how the organizations covered it up in plain view. For example, in 1956, the St. Louis Hawks drafted four black superstars: Julius McCoy (All-American, Michigan State), Wally Choice (Indiana), Willie Nulls (UCLA), and Bill Russell (San Francisco). The organization did not keep any of these prolific scorers!

In addition to that travesty, NBA teams were notorious for giving the players that did make it one-year contracts. It was generally only the black players who had to try out year after year. Can you imagine Kobe Bryant having to audition along with two hundred college kids every year for a position on the Los Angeles Lakers?

Even more telling is the fact that we're talking about being *signed* to a team and not actually *playing*. That was a whole other battle in itself. In 1950, Chuck Cooper was drafted in the second round from Duquesne University after his Army discharge. Nat "Sweetwater" Clifton (Xavier University) also came in that year by way of Abe, but it took awhile before he clocked any time on the court. Finally, Earl Lloyd (9th round Draft pick from West Virginia State) is the first to step foot on the court on Halloween 1950, the same year that Hank Dezoni (who we rarely hear about) received time in a game, although there is some discrepancy among ballplayers of that era as to who *truly* played first. Earl Lloyd and Jim Tucker were the first blacks in the NBA to win a NBA championship in 1955.

Another black player, Fred LaCour, hit the court a few months after Lloyd, allegedly because his complexion was so fair the NBA and everyone else thought he was white. It wasn't until his family members came to the game that they realized the truth and he was ultimately released from his contract.

"Elgin Baylor was the first black that was given the freedom to shoot the ball."—Andy Johnson

In 1955, the Philadelphia Warriors jumped on the bandwagon and added their first black player, a local college player by the name of Jackie Moore. After that, the Warriors were cautious with their entry, even with the direct access they had through Abe Saperstein. They still followed the unwritten rule of having a maximum of two black players per team. However, a few short years later, as the Civil Rights movement was at its height, it became clear that the face of the game was beginning to change. Andy Johnson was part of that change.

I can't think of a professional basketball team more suited for my dad than one named the Warriors. A warrior doesn't just fight, he's strategic in his approach. A warrior studies his opponent and does only what is necessary to conquer him, without any extra fanfare or dramatics. That's how Dad approached basketball. He was a strategist and he played the game with intelligence and precision. It wasn't necessary for Dad to show the world he could dunk forty different ways or score a million points, because he did what was necessary for the team to win according to what he was told. He was *coachable*, as they call it in the league. Sometimes that might mean score and sometimes that might mean assist, a statistic that wasn't consistently recorded on the published stats back then. Whatever it meant, my dad was a warrior before he ever set foot on the Philadelphia Warriors' court.

Wilt Chamberlin (Philly) and Tommy Heinsohn (Boston) fight it out in the Warrior-Celtic play-off game in which Wilt ended up with a broken hand. The Celtics ended up winning the series.

However, as with every other aspect of Dad's basketball career, his transition from the Harlem Globetrotters to the Philadelphia Warriors was negotiated without his input. , Dad was trapped under Abe. And, he wasn't alone.

The story of how Dad came to play for the Warriors starts with Abe Saperstein, who was partial owner of the Warriors. Saperstein longed to have his own team in the NBA. His plan was to duplicate the success he had with the all-black Trotters within the league, so he was always striving to build relationships with key people. In fact, at one point, Saperstein was promised ownership of the Lakers franchise. Abe had once owned part of the Warriors but sold his portion of the team to Eddie Gottlieb for $25,000, making Gottlieb the sole owner of the Warriors.

Saperstein wanted his own franchise team in the NBA, so he kept one bridge unburned: Eddie Gottlieb. In order to solidify his chances of owning a team, Saperstein would play the exhibition games every year but would never let his Trotters team win after the late forties so-called upset wins over the Lakers. He and Eddie had the relationship to start letting some of the Trotters in through the Philadelphia gateway. Dad was one of those players. Therefore, in 1958, Dad was *sold* to the Philadelphia Warriors as a starting forward. He was essentially half-Globetrotter, half-Warrior.

"You were still Abe's boy, even if you were playing somewhere else. They would loan us to anyone at any time."—Andy Johnson

Like most of the blacks who entered the NBA in the early years, Dad was given a role that he was expected to play. Philadelphia did not have anyone on its team to go up against people like Boston's Tom Heinsohn, who was known as one of the toughest players in the league (and who later became one of Dad's good friends). Part of Dad's role was also to stop the best scores. Because of Andy's build and roughness, he was supposed to pass the ball, get the rebound, and not let his team-mates or himself get beat up. But Dad was not to be a star. He was required to water down his abilities and not play *his* game. Instead he was supposed to play the game presented to him, and that game consisted of making the Warriors' "Big 3" look good, even if Andy was a better ballplayer.

Dad understood what was expected and, as in his past, he knew how to behave. He put a new spin on his name, Andy "The Enforcer" Johnson, by enforcing this new way of playing—not by making the "Big 3" look good, but by making them look great. Teams knew that if you were going to come to town and beat up the Warriors, you would have to go through the enforcer, Andy Johnson. This was, of course, to the detriment of Dad's own stats and the perception that others had of him as a true star.

In one amazing story that Dad told me, this fact became crystal clear. It was a really close game, the Warriors were down one point, and the coach called a time-out to instruct his team. He told Andy that if he should be passed the ball and none of the Big 3 was open, to throw the ball out of bounds. When the game started back up, Andy was thrown the ball by a teammate and, finally exhausted with not being able to play his game, he decided to teach the coach a lesson. The Big 3 were preoccupied defensively and he was wide open for the shot. So ... he threw the ball out of bounds. The buzzer rang loudly and the Warriors lost the game. The infuriated coach, with a severe case of short-term amnesia, asked Andy why he threw the ball. Dad answered firmly, "Because you told me to." They never asked him to do that again.

Woody Sauldsberry, the Warriors' 1957 NBA Rookie of the Year, shared this with me: "When Andy came to the NBA, we played together with the Warriors. He was already a star but, to me, he never wanted to rock the boat. His mentality changed. He did what they wanted him to do." Carl Green says Andy acted that way because Andy knew he had a family to feed at home; so he played his part as much as possible.

All the same, Dad's experience with the Warriors created lifelong friendships with players like Tom Gola, Paul Arizin, and Guy Rodgers, who'd previously played against him in several College All-Star games. He played basketball with these guys but they also became like brothers to him.

Sauldsberry continued, "Andy was the funniest guy I'd ever met. We were roommates and friends, but we were always in

Andy Did the Job

Andy Johnson did what he was supposed to do. He stopped **Dolph Schayes**, cold. As cold as any man ever stopped the great Syracuse forward.

But pro basketball is still a team game, and that's why the Nats are hot and the Warriors are cold.

Handy Andy, the muscular Tribe forward, played Schayes nose to nose for 25 minutes. And all dandy Dolph had to show for his run-run-run, hustle-hustle-hustle antics was one field goal—a layup in the fading seconds of play.

"**ANDY THREW** a blanket over me," Schayes said later. "He played me as tough as any man ever played me. It was like he was taking every step I took, only taking it before I took it. I couldn't shake him off."

Schayes, who picked up three baskets while being guarded by **Tom Gola**, wound up with 10 points and 10 rebounds. But Johnson's hawking his every move forced the 33-year-old NYU grad to lose the ball on traveling violations five times.

"I tried hard," Johnson said later. "But I guess I didn't try hard enough because we didn't win."

It wasn't Andy's fault.

STATISTICS STATIC: Wilt Chamberlain led both teams in scoring with 46 points and 32 rebounds, but the figures are misleading. Eleven of the points came in the final four minutes when the game was out of reach. In the earlier sections he was obviously bothered by the close, tough guarding of Swede Halbrook and a folding Nat defense. He missed several from the distance of a foot or less, but was not in every play. . . . Halbrook, who got a big hand from the partisan fans when he came out for the Warriors picked up 15 points, 15 in the fourth quarter, and knocked the ball away from Wilt six times, them leading to fast break baskets for the Warriors. . . . "That's the longest I've played (31 minutes) since I'm a member," the 7-3 center said. "I can't even remember playing this long in the NIBL. But I'm not tired when you win a big one . . . You're never . . . The Warriors got off 22 more shots than the Nats but made two less field goals. They also made more foul shots, but made two less. And the 76-58 bulge in the rebounding department is where the game was won. . . . the box score has no column for pressure and that's where the game was won." —JA

CONTINUED ON PAGE SEVENTY-NINE

The 55 Are Wilt's, But Game Is Andy's

By JACK KISER

CINCINNATI—When a guy scores 55 points and 29 rebounds, it would be a little ridiculous to single another player as the key figure in a victory wouldn't [it].

[Sure]. Yet Neil Johnston, Tom Marshall, Jack Twyman and Wilt Chamberlain all put the finger on a man [who] scored only 16 points and got four rebounds as the [big] factor in last night's 124-116 Warrior victory over [Cincin]nati.

[A]ND WHEN this quartet got through with their explanations, you'd have to admit that Handy Andy Johnson was indeed the turning point in a give-no-quarter battle.

Johnson, a 6-6 escapee from Abe Saperstein's hoop circus, pulled the sagging Warriors up by their willing sneaker straps with a sensational third-period whirlwind performance.

[To] set the stage:

[CHAM]BERLAIN, the guy (natch) who wound up [with the] 55-point, 29-rebound worksheet, had scored 28 [in the] opening half. Yet the keyed-up Royals held [him at] halftime bulge thanks mainly to a 19-point [scoring] effort by Twyman.

[Marshall] had tried Woody Sauldsberry, Guy Sparrow [and Jo]oski as defensive weapons against the sharp-[shooting] forward, only to see them flounder help-[lessly on] pick-off plays that sprung Twyman loose for [a field-goal] bander.

WILT CHAMBERLAIN
... what new marks to conquer?

Andy Key Man in Warrior Win

CONTINUED FROM PAGE SEVENTY-ONE

Andy, who had started the game in place of the ailing Sauldsberry but ran into foul trouble in the first period, bounced off the bench in the third quarter to score 13 points and hold Twyman to a pair of foul shots. Almost single-handedly, he pushed the Warriors into a 92-88 edge as the final 12 minutes started. And the Tribe was never headed after that.

MARSHALL, THE ROYALS' suffering coach, just shook his head sadly when mentally replaying the game. "We know that your big man (Wilt) is going to pile them in, but we were matching him basket for basket. Then that Johnson comes in and hits points we don't figure on. Besides that, he sticks to our big scorer so tight he can't get off a decent shot. Yes, I'd say that Andy was the difference tonight."

T w y m a n, who finally wound up with 32 points, was unusually generous with his praise. "Andy hounded me like a shadow," he said. "They'd set up picks for me and he would walk right over them. He's a bull of a man and he don't get discouraged easily."

JOHNSTON said practically the same thing. Except a little more eloquently. "How many players do you know who hold their head up in [...] ...

... the big plays
ANDY JOHNSON

same way. Well-wishers crowded around him. Pumping hols hand for setting a new Cincy Garden scoring record. "Thanks. I was lucky," he muttered. But you should shake the hand of that man over there (motioning toward Johnson). He is the one who got the big buckets."

Andy, a soft-spoken guy who seems ill at ease when

the praise comes his way, just scuffed at the floor with a shoe and tried to appear nonchalant. "Aw" he said, "I just had a lot of apologizin' to do for the bad games I've played."

* * *

FREE THROWS: The Warriors arrive back in Phil'— this afternoon and get a w. deserved rest before hosting Minneapolis tomorrow night . . . Chamberlain's 55 points were 12 better than his previous high, yet he says it came harder than any of the others. "I found it harder to get my offensive position out there than against anybody else," he said later.

NBA Standings

EASTERN DIVISION	W	L	Pct.	WESTERN DIVISION	W	L	Pct.
Boston	8	1	.889	St. Louis	4	2	.667
WARRIORS	7	1	.875	Detroit	4	7	.364
Syracuse	4	4	.500	Cincinnati	3	7	.300
New York	2	5	.286	Minn'polis	3	8	.273

YESTERDAY'S RESULTS
Detroit 107, Minneapolis 93
Syracuse 113, New York 104
WARRIORS 124, Cincinnati 116
(Only games scheduled)

WEEKEND SCHEDULE
TONIGHT—No game.
SATURDAY—Minneapolis vs. WARRIORS at Convention Hall; St. Louis at Boston; New York at Syracuse; Cincinnati at Detroit.
SUNDAY—WARRIORS at Minneapolis; Detroit at New York (TV); Boston at Cincinnati.

"Andy did what he was suppose to. He stopped Dolph Schayes, Cold. As cold as any man ever stopped the Great Syracuse forward."

103

NBA ALL STAR AWARD CEREMONIAL PICTURE

Back Row: Bill Russell, Willie Nauls, Tom Heinsohn, Hal Greer, Tom Gola, Wilt Chamberlain, Paul Arizin. Front Row: Richie Guerin, Dolph Schayes, Bob Cousy, Larry Costello and Red Auerbach.

competition with each other. We were both from California and went to all-white schools—him, North Hollywood and me, Compton, so we had that in common. But, we always argued. And our arguments always seemed to end up on the basketball court. I knew I could make him play me by saying 'You big awkward, clumsy ... I'm going to make you break your ankle. All of that gorilla stuff ain't going to work on me.' Andy would be so mad that all he'd do is just point to the gym. I remember that happened in Rome. We got into another argument and we couldn't wait until the sun came up to find a basketball court to play one on one."

The other team members also seemed to have nothing but respect for my dad. Andy Johnson didn't have to be the star of the show, averaging 20 to 25 points a game, although he did receive his share of press and prestige. Dad was the backbone of the team. He did what he was asked to do. In one game, he held one of the top scorers of the decade, NBA Hall of Famer Dolph Shayes, to zero points. This is when Dad picked up the name *Handy Andy*.

It makes me proud when I hear my "adopted aunt" Gladis Rogers (former wife of NBA unsung hero Guy Rogers) say, "It was so exciting when the famous announcer Dave Zinkoff would announce your dad coming into the game. Over the antiquated speaker system you would hear 'ANNNNDDYY JOHNNNNSON!' The way your dad strolled on the court with confidence, you knew something exciting was going to happen."

Too bad they never asked Dad to score! When he did score, the other team was in trouble. Carl Green recounted when he first saw Andy play. He and Jack DeFares were both stand out players for Winston Salem State—Mr. DaFares was named best player in NYC two years in a row along with having many 30-40 pt. games being named of the 25 best in CIAA history. They both, uncharacteristically they admitted when they saw Andy Johnson play, asked each other, "Who the hell is this guy?" Green said he had never seen some of the moves and dunks that Andy executed when he was allowed to do so.

Andy Johnson provided support for the team and he made others shine. Dad was known to stand up for his teammates in every way. And, as a result, some of his own teammates, even the ones who didn't get a chance to see him in action as a Trotter, still saw his talent. One of Dad's teammates, Ernie Beck, guard for

PHILADELPHIA VS. NEW YORK

Wilt Chamberlain (Philadelphia Warrior #13) grabs the rebound from Charlie Tyra (New York Knicks #9), as Andy Johnson (Philadelphia Warrior #12) and Paul Arzin (Philadelphia Warrior #11) look on.

the Warriors from 1953 to 1960, said, "Andy Johnson was a very good defender and although he was only six feet, five inches, he helped us a lot in the low post. He was very strong and tough. He was the kind of guy you didn't want to mess with."

In the 1950s, the players had to be rough. Some white guys were not thrilled about playing alongside black players and would often attempt to beat up the black players in the name of defense. Some referees would turn a blind eye to what was happening; unlike today, there were hardly any suspensions or heavy fines. Thus, the first blacks in the league had to be quick and assertive just to avoid being beat to a pulp by elbows to the ribs and charges to the chest.

Dad said there were times when the referees called fouls on him and he was on the bench. The refs probably did not like some of the things Andy said to them; for example, Dad once told a ref to "take that Klu Klux Klan whistle out of your mouth." Quite harsh, yes, but probably well deserved.

Dad had some of his front teeth knocked out while playing in one of these early games, and Wilt Chamberlain had his teeth put through his lips once. My father would talk about the great Maurice Stokes, who was the 1955 NBA Rookie of the Year while playing for the Rochester Royals. In 1958, in one of the last games of the season in Minneapolis, Stokes received a hard back-in-the-day foul and went to the floor and hit his head. He was knocked unconscious. After he was revived, he returned to the game. A few days later, after an outstanding performance in Detroit against the Pistons, he became ill, fell into a coma, and was left permanently paralyzed. He died a few years later from a heart attack at the age of thirty-six. He was diagnosed with "post-traumatic encephalopathy, a brain injury that damaged his motor control center. At the time, some in the media wanted the public to believe that Stokes' career ended because he was bit by an insect and that was what caused his injury. But others, like my dad, believe it was because of all the abuse on the court.

Dad saw this "accepted" behavior in the NBA, especially against the first African Americans in the league. He decided to exhibit a way of playing by the rules, but not letting anyone beat him up in the process. This is why Andy was known as The Enforcer. You were not going to beat him or any of his teammates.

Oftentimes, Dad would say to me, "They are not going to make me the Jackie Robinson story." I never understood what he meant until I saw the 1950 movie directed by Alfred E. Green in which Jackie Robinson played himself. He was told by the organization no matter what someone says or does to you, you can't fight back. Then it was clear. Dad wasn't going to agree not to stand his ground or fight back if he felt he was being mistreated.

This reminds me of one of the many games Dad would reminisce about. While playing in a game, every time he went for a rebound the player from the opposing team would hit Dad across the face. And every time he did, he would say, "Excuse me; I am sorry."

After the third time, Dad said he turned around and punched the guy in the face. The player looked at him and said, "Andy, what are you doing?" Dad replied, "I am fighting. And, by the way, excuse me and I am sorry."

One night, when the Warriors were playing New York, a riot broke out. It was toward the end of the game and Philadelphia was down two points and had to get the ball back. The coach told dad to give New York Knicks' Richie Guerin a hard foul. After Dad fouled the player, Guerin's face turned beet red in anger. Dad politely said to him, "What's wrong with you?"

Guerin replied in a growling voice, "I am a Marine."

Andy Johnson's classic response was, "But this is the NBA, not the service." The next thing you know, Guerin leaps for Dad. Wrong move. He must not have known about Andy's short boxing career. Guy Sparrow jumped in, followed by Woody Sauldsberry, and soon everyone was involved. The fight spilled onto the front row, benches tumbled, and even the fans had some of the players in headlocks. I don't know if there were any fines issued but it really gave the fans something to talk about!

Fights broke out all the time in the early NBA. Players had five fouls and they used them wisely and usually very aggressively. Boston's Jim Luskatoff threw an elbow in one game and knocked all of Dad's front teeth out, but Dad wasn't intimidated by that. He knew the league wouldn't run to a black player's aid when it came to abuse. He played the game as it presented itself and in turn, he made other players think really hard about whether they wanted to play basketball or whether they wanted to fight.

Because of his mild manner off the court and his no-nonsense attitude on the court, Dad learned how to adapt and build bridges between players in the league and in his community. He became a Philly favorite and remained one for most of his life. Because of his attitude and spirit, the brotherly love and admiration that defined Dad's tenure with the Trotters continued when he became a Warrior.

The friendships and camaraderie extended across team lines, as well. Often the black players of the opposing team would invite Dad and the other black players on the Warriors to dinner when they played against each other. It was clarified by Barbara Chamberlain Lewis (Wilt's sister) that Wilt would always invite Bill Russell, K.C. Jones and sometimes Sam Jones over for dinner, when they played in Philadelphia; but as Dad explained, these invites were a way for black ballplayers to get a home-cooked meal and escape, if only for an evening, the racist world in which they lived and played.

However, not all of the black players were best friends. Dad had a habit of exposing some of the greats and holding them to their responsibility as professionals. During one of the games, Philadelphia versus Los Angeles, Elgin Baylor asked Dad, "Why are you playing me so hard?" Dad told him to look up in the stands. "You see all those kids? Well, this might be the only time they get the chance to see the Great Elgin Baylor!"

Most of the players in the league respected Andy Johnson, and some were his friends and co-workers. But the fact still remains that before there was an Elgin Baylor in Los Angeles, there was Andy Johnson. Before there was a Michael Jordan in Chicago, there was Andy Johnson; and from his own mouth, before there was a Wilt Chamberlain in Philadelphia, there was Andy Johnson.

9

A Day in the Life
of a Warrior

MY FATHER ALWAYS TAUGHT ME TO RESPECT EVERYBODY. He said it didn't matter if the person was two years old or ninety-two years old; that you can learn from everyone and anyone could say something that would change your life. I believe Dad learned this in a much more difficult way, a way that challenged him as a man but also changed how he dealt with the coaches and owners that took advantage of him. He decided that if he couldn't challenge them on paper and in contracts, he'd use what he always had, his talent, to get the smaller things he needed and desired. One day in particular, this became crystal clear to Dad.

Even though Andy Johnson was the star player on the Philadelphia Warriors, he had six mouths to feed and couldn't afford a car to get back and forth to home games. Never one to complain, he simply took public transportation to the game. Yes, one of the top professional basketball players in the city, and arguably in the league, took the Septa city bus to his games. I know it would be unimaginable in today's world to see Shaquille O'Neal or Michael Jordan on the Number 12 bus to the United Center, but this *was* Andy Johnson's reality. Andy did not have agents working tirelessly on his behalf.

In fact, the one time he decided to consult an attorney regarding his contract, Eddie Gottlieb said, rather pointedly, to Andy, "So, where are you and your attorney going to play basketball?" In other words, you play according to his rules or nobody's rules. And for a little while, Dad played that game; until one spring day when he boarded a city bus to the stadium. With his Philadelphia Warriors bag in hand, Andy sat near the back of the bus in his usual fashion. A young boy, no more than six years old, was sitting with his mom. She pointed at Dad and said, "There goes one of the Philadelphia Warriors, sweetie." The little boy smiled back at Dad and then innocently turned to his mother and said, "That's not one of the Warriors, Mom. Why would he be riding a bus with us?"

That's when Andy's eyes opened to the reality of his situation. It wasn't that he thought himself better than anyone else that took public transportation, but he considered the enormous amount of money he was bringing to the team owners— as he had for all of the teams that he'd played on—money that could have easily made sure he could get to the games quickly. The little boy was right and it took his youthful observation to make Andy Johnson realize that, no matter what, one of the premier basketball players in the city shouldn't be getting to the games via city bus. He presented that fact to Gottlieb, as he walked into the office and bluntly said, "I need a car."

The ironic thing was, Gottlieb, knowing the strong will of Andy Johnson when it came to the obvious, never fought him on it; proving yet another lesson that Dad shared with me—you don't get what you don't ask for. In fact, Dad and Gottlieb immediately went down to the Buick dealership on Broad Street and, like the other times, Dad signed his name and they gave him a car. The whole process didn't take more than an hour.

This was one of the first times that a player knocked on the owner's door over how he was getting treated. It didn't make sense that players who were being featured in advertisements and promotions had to take public transportation to the game. With people like my father standing up, it became easier for others to demand equal treatment.

When Wilt Chamberlain came to the Warriors, he walked right through the door. He was the first to demand one of the largest contracts of that day, not only for African Americans in the league but for all players. If players like Dad opened the door, players like Wilt kicked it down.

Dad always showed me, through his stories, a very important reality: People do whatever they want to do. We run into it every day. You're on the phone with a customer service representative who is giving you a hard time and as soon as you put a little pressure on him by asking for the supervisor, all of a sudden, things can get done. As a young person, I used to question why people didn't just do what they knew was right the first time around. Dad would simply say, "You didn't ask them to." I think he was right.

The one thing Andy Johnson never forgot was the notion of being an ambassador of goodwill. Dad would hold free basketball clinics for the kids of Philadelphia and always gave back to the community, not because he was going to get some kind of an award or because it was mandated by the NBA. He and Woody helped create the Baker League for the youths of Philadelphia with Charles Baker and Sonny Hill. This league still functions today, under the direction of another great Philadelphia basketball local, Sonny Hill. Dad was a professional who was accessible and he felt it was important for him to remain that way.

The Sunday Bulletin Philadelphia, Sunday, August 14, 1960 S G   7

'Sorry, Honey! This Clinic Isn't for Sick Little Dolls'

The "young mother" clutching her doll babies at the r ight seems a bit bewildered with the happenings at Lanier Playground, 29th and Tasker sts. But the grou ip of boys gathered around Warriors' player Andy Johnson (on sliding board) aren't confused. When play ground instructor Jerry Rullo (right foreground), a former Warrior, announced that Johnson was going to s top at Lanier to conduct one of his series of basketball clinics for the Department of Recreation boys wer e ready and anxious.

Dad appeared at public places for free—when it was not mandatary—as it sometimes is part of a player's contract today.

10

SOLD Again! Now What?

THE 1959-60 PHILADELPHIA WARRIORS ROSTER included some of the top scorers of the NBA, plus Andy Johnson and Wilt Chamberlain. Most of the players from the previous year had returned and the coaches were starting to let Dad have a little more freedom; and Wilt had a fantastic rookie year. This team was poised to finally beat the seemingly unstoppable Boston Celtics for the World Championship.

It was all coming together. The stage was set. It was Boston against Philly in the finals of the Eastern Division. Boston had taken a 3 to 2 lead in the series, but Philly was confident they would beat Boston because they'd won the previous game by a 20-point margin. Unfortunately, Philadelphia lost the next and final game to Boston by two points and Boston advanced to the

NBA finals to meet and beat the St. Louis Hawks for the NBA world championship.

The loss devastated everyone in Philadelphia; but like all professional sports, basketball was a business. It was time to move on and start planning for the next season. While the players and coaches focused on how to win a championship the following year, the name and the game for the NBA was about expansion and seizing untapped markets. The league had dwindled down to eight teams. This is how they functioned for several years. The NBA set its sights on Chicago. The last team in Chicago had been the Chicago Stags, which was dismantled by the 1950-51 season, leaving the city without a professional basketball team for nearly ten years. Who better to assist the NBA with this task but Abe Saperstein?

When they asked Abe for his assistance, he jumped at the opportunity. It was the kind of break that had to turn into a favor, one that Abe had been waiting for a long time. You see, he still wanted a franchise team. They promised Abe his own team in Los Angeles in exchange for helping establish a new franchise team. Abe was a Chicago native, and that is where the Harlem Globetrotters' office was located. He felt like this was his chance to get what he wanted from the NBA. Abe had the players and the clout to help build a franchise in his hometown. So, it was one hand washing the other to obtain a franchise. Besides, Abe had made many friends in the NBA, or so he thought, by having all those exhibition games and the double-headers to sustain the NBA in its early years.

Abe thought he could finalize the deal by "loaning" the players Chicago knew could draw a crowd. What players were better to loan than former Globetrotters like Andy Johnson and Woody Sauldsberry, who already had a following in the Chicago area? And, this was where things get shady . . . Andy and Woody were different kinds of players. They did not have the subservient attitude that most of the black players had before and around them and that the white owners expected. It is rather like the example of the house nigga compared to the field nigga, where the house nigga was well-behaved and could come inside the house. And if the slave master felt as though he could not trust or properly control a slave, the slave would be confined to work in the fields and not allowed in the house. Woody was very outspoken about how blacks were treated in the league and Andy was not going to let anyone beat him up. He fought back, and most of the time it was real physical. These were some of the reasons why they went to the expansion team in Chicago.

You see, NBA contracts were notoriously known to be slave-like agreements. A strong analogy; but if you take a close look at the verbiage of the contract my dad had with the Warriors you will see it was written totally on the behalf and favor of the NBA. Not many players had the option to put attorneys on retainer or had agents working on their behalf. There were several questionable clauses in the contracts of the era. One in particular, that was exercised with my father, was that a player could be "loaned" to another team. Can you imagine your favorite player being loaned to another team, at any given time?

Abe could decide where his "property" played. Even though they were under NBA contracts, the Trotters were still Abe's property. This is actually how Dad and Woody ended up in Philadelphia in the beginning. You see, the Minneapolis Lakers wanted Dad really badly after he put on a 37-point performance

NATIONAL BASKETBALL ASSOCIATION

UNIFORM PLAYER CONTRACT

THIS AGREEMENT made this __6__ day of __Aug__ 19__60__ by and between __Chicago Packers Inc__ (hereinafter called the Club), a member of the National Basketball Association, and __Andrew Johnson__ of the City, Town of __Chicago__ (hereinafter called the Player).

WITNESSETH:—

In consideration of the several and/or mutual promises and/or agreements hereinafter contained, the parties hereto promise and agree as follows:

1. The Club hereby employs the Player as a skilled Basketball Player for the term of one year from the 1st day of October 19__ The Player's employment shall include attendance at training camp, playing the games scheduled for the team during the schedule season of the National Basketball Association, playing all exhibition games scheduled by the team during and prior to the schedule season, and playing the playoff games for which the player is to receive such additional compensation as is provided by the Association. Regular players will not be required to attend training camp earlier than four weeks prior to the season starting date of the team of which the player is a member. "Rookies" may be required to attend training camp at an earlier date. Exhibition games shall not be played on the three days prior to the opening of a team's regular season schedule nor on a day prior to a regularly scheduled game. The All-Star game shall for the purpose of this paragraph not be considered an exhibition game. Exhibition games during the regularly scheduled season shall not exceed three.

2. The club agrees to pay the Player for rendering services described herein the sum of $__11,000__ in twelve equal semi-monthly payments beginning with the first of said payments on November 15th of the season above described and continuing with such payments on the first and fifteenth of each month until said sum is paid in full. Provided however if the Club does not qualify for the playoffs the payments due subsequent to the conclusion of the schedule season shall become due and payable immediately after the conclusion of the schedule season.

3. The Club promises and agrees to pay the reasonable board and lodging expenses of the Player while playing for the Club in other than the Club's home city and will pay all proper and necessary expenses of the Player and his meals enroute. Each basketball player, while "on the road," shall be paid seven dollars ($7.00) per day as meal expense allowance.

4. The club may from time to time during the continuance of this contract establish reasonable rules for the government of its players "at home" and "abroad," and such rules shall be a part of this contract as fully as if herein written and shall be binding upon the player; and for violation of such rules or for any conduct impairing the faithful and thorough discharge of the duties incumbent upon the player, the club may impose reasonable fines upon the player and deduct the amount thereof from any money due or to become due to the player. The club may also suspend the player for violation of any rules so established, and during such suspension the player shall not be entitled to any compensation under this contract. When the player is fined or suspended, he shall be given notice in writing, stating the amount of the fine or the duration of the suspension and the reason therefor.

__ Basketball Association to fail, refuse or neglect faithfully to discharge his duties thereunder, or interfere in any manner whatsoever with the operation or conduct of the business of the said Association or of any member thereof. For any violation of this Paragraph 4a, the Club and the President of the said Association shall each have the concurrent right and power to terminate this contract forthwith, or the President of the said Association shall deem appropriate, and the President of the said Association shall have the additional right and power in his sole discretion to expel the Player, or to suspend him for a definite or an indefinite period, as a player for any member of the said Association. The Club shall have the right to deduct from any money due or to become due to the Player the amount of any fine imposed hereunder and the Player shall not be entitled to any compensation under this contract during the period of any suspension hereunder. Any fine or suspension hereunder shall be imposed by notice in writing delivered or mailed to the Player, stating the amount of the fine, the duration of the suspension and the reason therefor and the Player shall be entitled to no other notice or hearing in connection therewith.

5. The Player promises and agrees (a) to report at the time and place fixed by the Club in good physical condition; and (b) to keep himself throughout the entire season in good physical condition; and (c) to give his best services, as well as his loyalty, to the Club, and to play basketball only for the Club unless released, sold or exchanged by the Club; and (d) to be neatly and fully attired in public and always to conduct himself on and off the court according to the highest standards of honesty, morality, fair play and sportsmanship; and (e) not to do anything which is detrimental to the best interests of the Club or of the National Basketball Association or of professional sports.

5a. In addition to his services in connection with the actual playing of basketball, the Player agrees to cooperate with the Club and participate in any and all promotional activities of the Club and the Association, which, in the opinion of the Club, will promote the welfare of the Club or professional basketball, and to observe and comply with all requirements of the Club respecting conduct and service of its teams and its players, at all times whether on or off the playing floor.

6. If the Player, in the sole judgment of the Club's physician, is not in good physical condition at the date of his first scheduled game for the Club, or if, during the season, he fails to remain in good physical condition, unless such condition results directly from playing basketball for the Club, so as to render him, in the sole judgment of the Club's physician unfit to play skilled basketball, it is mutually agreed that the Club shall have the right to suspend such Player until such time as, in the sole judgment of the Club's physician, the Player is in sufficiently good physical condition to play skilled basketball, and in the event of such suspension, the annual sum payable to the Player shall be proportionately reduced as the length of the period of disability, during which, in the sole judgment of the Club's physician, the Player is unfitted to play skilled basketball, bears to the length of the season. If the Player is injured as a direct result of participating in any basketball practice or game played for the Club, the Club will pay the Player's reasonable hospitalization until he is discharged from the hospital and his reasonable medical expenses and doctor's bills, provided the hospital and the doctor are selected by the Club, and provided further, that the Club's obligation to pay said medical expenses and said doctor's bills shall terminate at a period not exceeding eight weeks (8) after the injury. It is also agreed that if the Player's said injury or injuries resulting directly from playing for the Club render him, in the sole judgment of the Club's physician, unfit to play skilled basketball for the balance of the season or any part thereof, then during such time as the Player is unfit to play skilled basketball, but in no event beyond the period described in paragraph 1, the Club shall pay the Player the compensation hereinbefore provided for and the Player releases the Club from any and every additional obligation or liability, claim and demand whatsoever.

7. The Player agrees to give to the Club's coach or the Club's physician (a) written or verbal notice of any minor injury suffered by him as soon as possible, but in any event, within forty-eight (48) hours thereafter; and (b) written notice of any major injury sustained by the Player as soon as possible, but in any event within four (4) days after the sustaining of such injury, such notice to state the time, place, cause and nature of said injury.

8. Should the player become disabled as provided in the preceding section, he will submit himself to a medical examination and treatment by a regular physician, in good standing, to be selected by the Club. Such examination when made at the request of the Club shall be at its expense, unless made necessary by some act or conduct of the player contrary to the terms of this agreement or rules and regulations made under it.

9. The Player represents and agrees that he has exceptional and unique skill and ability as a basketball player; that his services

10. It is mutually agreed that the Club shall have the right to sell, exchange, assign and transfer this contract, to loan the Player's services to any other Professional Basketball Club and the Player agrees to accept such assignment and to faithfully perform and carry out this contract with the same force and effect as if it had been entered into by the Player with the assignee Club instead of with this Club.

10. (a) It is mutually agreed that, in the event that the Player's contract is sold, exchanged, assigned or transferred to any other Professional Basketball Club, all reasonable expenses incurred by the Player in moving himself and his family from the home City of the Club to the home City of the Club to which such sale, exchange, assignment or transfer is made, as a result thereof, shall be paid by the assignee Club.

11. It is mutually agreed that, in the event that the Player's contract is assigned to another Club the Player shall be forthwith notified, by a notice in writing, delivered to the Player personally or delivered or mailed to his last known address and the Player shall report to the assignee Club within forty-eight hours after said written notice has been personally delivered or received at his last known address or within such longer time for reporting as may be specified in said written notice. If Player does not report to the Club to which his contract has been assigned within the aforesaid time, Player may be suspended, by either Club and he shall lose the sums which would otherwise be payable to him as long as the suspension lasts.

12. It is mutually agreed that the Club will not pay and the Player will not accept any bonus or anything of value for winning any particular Association game.

13. It is severally and mutually agreed that the only contracts which shall be recognized by the President of the National Basketball Association are those which have been duly executed and filed in the Association's office and approved by him.

These contracts were given to players with no representation.

14. The Player and the Club expressly acknowledge that the President and the Board of Governors of the National Basketball Association is and may be empowered by present and future provisions of the Constitution and By-Laws and action of said Association to impose fines upon the Player and/or upon the Club for causes and in the manner provided in such Constitution and By-Laws and such action. The Player and the Club, each for himself and itself, promise promptly to pay to the said Association each and every fine imposed upon him or it in accordance with the said provisions of said Constitution and By-Laws and not to permit any such fine to be paid on his or its behalf by anyone other than the person or Club fined. The player further authorizes the Club to deduct any fines imposed on or assessed against him from his salary payments.

15. Notwithstanding any provision of the Constitution or of the By-Laws of the National Basketball Association, it is agreed that if the President of the National Basketball Association shall in his sole judgment find that the Player has bet, or has offered or attempted to bet, money or anything of value on the outcome of any game participated in by any club which is a member of the National Basketball Association, the President shall have the power in his sole discretion to suspend the Player indefinitely or to expel him as a player for any member of the National Basketball Association, and the President's finding and decision shall be final, binding, conclusive and unappealable; and the Player hereby releases the President and waives every claim he may have against the President and/or the National Basketball Association, and against every Club in the National Basketball Association, and against every director, officer and stockholder of every Club in the National Basketball Association, for damages and for all claims and demands whatsoever arising out of or in connection with the decision of the President of the National Basketball Association.

16. The Player and the Club recognize and agree that the Player's participation in other sports may impair or destroy his ability and skill as a basketball player. The player and the Club recognize and agree that the Player's participation in basketball out of season may result in injury to him. Accordingly the Player agrees that he will not engage in professional boxing or wrestling; and that, except with the written consent of the Club, he will not engage in any game or exhibition of basketball, football, baseball, hockey, lacrosse, or other athletic sport, under penalty of such fine and suspension as may be imposed by the Club and/or the President of the Association.

17. The Player agrees that his picture and pictures of his team in play may be taken for still photographs, motion pictures or television at such times as the Club may designate and agrees that all rights in such pictures shall belong to the Club and may be used by the Club in any manner it desires. The Player further agrees that during the playing season he will not make public appearances, participate in radio or television programs or permit his picture to be taken or write or sponsor newspaper or magazine articles or sponsor commercial products without the written consent of the Club, which shall not be withheld except in the reasonable interests of the Club or professional basketball.

18. The player agrees and covenants that during the life of this contract he will not tamper with or enter into negotiations with any other player under contract or reservation to any Club, which is a member of this Association, for, or regarding, his future or present services without written consent of the Club of which the Player negotiated with is a member, under penalty of a fine.

19. (a) The Player may terminate this contract, upon written notice to the Club, if the Club shall default in the payments to the Player provided for in paragraph 2 hereof or shall fail to perform any other obligation agreed to be performed by the Club hereunder and if the Club shall fail to remedy such default within ten (10) days after the receipt by the Club of written notice of such default. The Player may also terminate this contract as provided in sub-paragraph (f)(4) of this paragraph 19.

(b) The Club may terminate this contract upon written notice to the Player (but only after requesting and obtaining waivers of this contract from all other Clubs) if the Player shall at any time:

(1) fail, refuse or neglect to conform his personal conduct to the standards of good citizenship and good sportsmanship or to keep himself in first class physical condition or to obey the Club's training rules; or

(2) fail, in the opinion of the Club's management, to exhibit sufficient skill or competitive ability to qualify to continue as a member of the Club's team; or

(3) fail, refuse or neglect to render his services hereunder or in any other manner materially breach this contract.

(c) If this contract is terminated by the Club by reason of the Player's failure to render his services hereunder due to disability resulting directly from injury sustained in the course and within the scope of his employment hereunder and written notice of such injury is given to the Player as provided herein, the Player shall be entitled to receive his full salary for the season in which the injury was sustained, less all workmen's compensation payments paid or payable by reason of said injury.

---

19. (a) The Player may terminate this contract, upon written notice to the Club, if the Club shall default in the payments to the Player provided for in paragraph 2 hereof or shall fail to perform any other obligation agreed to be performed by the Club hereunder and if the Club shall fail to remedy such default within ten (10) days after the receipt by the Club of written notice of such default. The Player may also terminate this contract as provided in sub-paragraph (f)(4) of this paragraph 19.

(b) The Club may terminate this contract upon written notice to the Player (but only after requesting and obtaining waivers of this contract from all other Clubs) if the Player shall at any time:

(1) fail, refuse or neglect to conform his personal conduct to the standards of good citizenship and good sportsmanship or to keep himself in first class physical condition or to obey the Club's training rules; or

(2) fail, in the opinion of the Club's management, to exhibit sufficient skill or competitive ability to qualify to continue as a member of the Club's team; or

(3) fail, refuse or neglect to render his services hereunder or in any other manner materially breach this contract.

(c) If this contract is terminated by the Club by reason of the Player's failure to render his services hereunder due to disability resulting directly from injury sustained in the course and within the scope of his employment hereunder and written notice of such injury is given to the Player as provided herein, the Player shall be entitled to receive his full salary for the season in which the injury was sustained, less all workmen's compensation payments paid or payable by reason of said injury.

(d) If this contract is terminated by the Club during the training season, payment by the Club of the Player's board, lodging and expense allowance during the training season to the date of termination and of the reasonable traveling expenses of the Player to his home city and the expert training and coaching provided by the Club to the Player during the training season shall be full payment to the Player.

(e) If this contract is terminated by the Club during the playing season, except in the case provided for in Sub-Paragraph (c) of this Paragraph 19, the Player shall be entitled to receive as full payment hereunder a sum of money which, when added to the salary which he has already received during the season, will represent the same proportionate amount of the total sum set forth in Paragraph 2 hereof as the number of days of the season then past bear to the total number of days of the playing season, plus the reasonable travelling expense of the Player to his home.

(f) If the Club proposes to terminate this contract in accordance with sub-paragraph (b) of this paragraph 19, the procedure shall be as follows:

(1) The Club shall request waivers from all other clubs. Such waiver request must state that it is for the purpose of terminating this contract and it may not be withdrawn.

(2) Upon receipt of the waiver request, any other club may claim assignment of this contract at such waiver price as may be fixed by the Association, the priority of claims to be determined in accordance with the Association Rules.

(3) If this contract is so claimed, the Club shall, promptly and before any assignment, notify the Player that it had requested waivers for the purpose of terminating this contract and that the contract had been claimed.

(4) Within 5 days after receipt of notice of such claim, the Player shall be entitled, by written notice to the Club, to terminate this contract on the date of his notice of termination. If the Player fails so to notify the Club, this contract shall be assigned to the claiming club.

(5) If the contract is not claimed, the Club shall promptly deliver written notice of termination to the Player at the expiration of the waiver period.

(g) Upon any termination of this contract by the Player, all obligations of both parties hereunder shall cease on the date of termination, except the obligation of the Club to pay the Player's compensation to said date.

EXAMINE THIS CONTRACT CAREFULLY BEFORE SIGNING IT.

RECEIVED & RECORDED

IN WITNESS WHEREOF the Player has hereunto set his hand and seal and the Club has caused this contract to be executed by its duly authorized officer.

AUG 15 1962

WITNESSES:

President.

Player.

Player's Address

This contract was signed in the beginning of the 62-63 season, anticipating Andy's return.
When they did not put him on waivers, no other team could pick him up.

119

on January 3, 1958, against them in one of those famed exhibition games, right before he entered the NBA. But, because of Abe's relationship with Warriors owner, Eddie Gottlieb, both Dad and Woody ended up in Philadelphia. So, now was no different. The deal was made and Andy and Woody went off to the new expansion team, the Chicago Packers.

Sadly, negotiations were made to make this "deal" before my father realized the depths of what was occurring. To a certain extent, Dad had some level of obligation, but remember, like the article said, "Sold to the Warriors." Philadelphia agreed to give Dad up because they now had Wilt to draw the crowds. In today's terms, Dad would be considered a "franchise player." Even though Andy was considered one of the "untouchables"—a player that was not supposed to be traded or loaned from the Warriors—to make the deal work, Abe exercised the rights of the contract and loaned Andy to Chicago to help the newly formed franchise.

Like all great deals, this one did not happen overnight. Abe had his sights set on a new team long before the last exhibition game in January 1958 between Los Angeles and the Globetrotters. These games between the NBA and the Trotters had been going on for almost ten years; little did anyone know this would be the last. When Abe put this particular game together it had to be different from all the rest. He knew he was moving closer than he had ever been to obtaining ownership of a team in the NBA. The league was growing and players were starting to bypass him and go directly into the NBA.

It was a rule that a player could not enter the NBA until his class graduated, which is one of the ways Abe gained control of all of the exceptional black players. He would go to these young men while they were still in college and recruit them by giving them what they thought was a lot of money and selling them dreams before they could finish school and be recruited by the NBA. Sound familiar? The NBA now recruits players out of high school. What kind of education are they ever going to obtain?

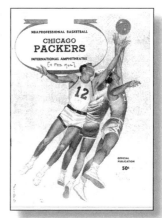

Remember, Abe was a visionary and he saw the direction that the NBA was heading, thanks to his assistance. But, he knew that the NBA still had its unwritten rule about the integration of the league. Abe knew he could not go into the exhibition game and beat the world champions by thirty or forty points, as they were used to doing to other teams. The serious ball players sometimes would not listen to Abe and run the score up anyway. He knew he had to be careful or the NBA would not let him put an *all-black team* in the league, especially if they thought that team would dominate the league.

So, as Carl Green explained, "Abe watered down the team." He did not allow all of the best Trotters to participate in that exhibition game. "It was also about control with Abe," added Green. "He knew he had the cream of the crop and he was going to maximize it to the best of his ability."

Yet even with the watered-down team, the Trotters started to dominate the Lakers. During the game, Abe called a time-out and made it clear to all of his players that if they were going to win it could not be by a large margin; so, the Trotters eventually lost.

Mission accomplished, right? Abe had helped Chicago by loaning them two of his greatest Trotters to draw the crowd. He held an exciting exhibition game that was played between the

Trotters and the Lakers—and the Trotters lost the game so the NBA wouldn't view them as a threat, or so he thought. All Abe had to do was sit back and wait until the LA franchise became available in the early 1960s.

As the 1961-62 season started with Chicago, Dad played incredibly well. His stats show he scored in the double digits in most games and defensively ruled the court. Playing along-side Walt Bellamy (NBA Hall of Fame), it was Andy Johnson who fed his phenomenal scoring; often passing for over twenty assists a game. Bellamy had to miss a few games because of a death in the family and Andy Johnson filled in. At an early televised game, Andy scored 42 points in the paint against top NBA player Swede Holbrook of the Syracuse Nationals.

Many times that season Andy took advantage of the opportunity to show what he had. In one game against Los Angeles, Elgin Baylor called to one of his teammates and said, "Gimme the ball. I have a lemon." He was referring to Dad. In true Andy Johnson fashion, Dad replied, "That's funny. I was thinking the same thing." In that game, Mr. Baylor found out just who Andy Johnson was.

In an interview with the *Philadelphia Daily News*, Dad discussed the season. "Our last game with Boston, Bill Russell comes over and shakes my hand and tells me what a fine season I've had and how I've improved, and how I'd finally found my place in basketball." Russell did not realize that Andy was a modest individual and the coaches were finally starting to allow him to play his game.

Andy played so well that the president of the organization approached him about signing his contract at the end of the season. This was unheard of; typically black players had to try out *every* year for a spot on the team. This signing was a testament to the performance that he displayed, not just in accumulating assists, but also in high scoring.

I can only imagine how good Andy was feeling. He was starting to make a stable atmosphere in which he felt comfortable and was getting recognition as a scorer. He was back in Chicago, along with Mom, where she grew up. The pre-season started and Dad went to camp, where they had open scrimmages. He went on a 30-point scoring frenzy. One day after practice, Dad said the coach called him into the office. He thought the coach was going to tell him what a great job he was doing. As the door closed, the coach told Dad that the team was letting him go and putting him on waivers. He said they couldn't use him and that he did not know the plays. Dad said they were old plays that he had learned when he first came into the league. So, he packed his bag and was on his way.

It was strange. He was the third-leading scorer on the Chicago team; yet it was the fourth-leading scorer, Sihugo Green, who returned. In Bob Cousy's 1963 Basketball magazine and in the sports sections of the major Chicago daily newspapers, articles anticipating Andy's return were published . . . and then nothing.

What happened? The headlines in the sports section of newspapers across the city screamed: "Andy Johnson's Release a Mystery!"

What did happen? Around the same time, the headlines also announced: "Owner of the Minneapolis Lakers, Bob Short, was permitted to move the Lakers to Los Angeles." Abe found out and was furious. So, Abe took his ball and went home! The NBA—in spite of all that Abe Saperstein had done for it—the latest being to help get Chicago off the ground—decided not to honor their agreement with him. They were not going to give him the team he was promised.

As a result, Abe did everything in his power to reverse all of the help he had given to the NBA. He immediately cancelled all doubleheaders and exhibition games. Last but not least, he began disputes over Dad's contract with the NBA. Andy Johnson was still partially signed with Abe, who did not want any of *his* (note the ownership) players with the Chicago organization. So, quite simply, he took his players back.

Woody Sauldsberry had not signed a contract with Chicago the year before and was able to slip through the cracks and go onto the St. Louis Hawks. But later he also had contract disputes, no doubt from Abe, and eventually left the NBA.

According to the NBA contract, if a team is sold or dismantled, or if a player is let go, they give a waiver to the player who's been contracted for that year so that the player might be picked up by another team. However, Dad had signed that contract and because of his affiliation with Abe Saperstein, the NBA did NOT honor their own contract and did not put Dad on waivers as a contractual agreement. Without a waiver, no team in the NBA could touch him. Even in today's contracts, players must be put on waivers or no other team can pick up their contract.

Several teams tried to pick up Andy. Who wouldn't? He'd just had a fantastic year in Chicago and a spectacular fan base in Philadelphia, along with his background with the Trotters. But no team could touch him without him being put on waivers. When Andy tried to retrieve his contract from the NBA, they would not give it to him. To top it off, they never even paid him for the signed contract.

Tommy's Corner

by TOMMY PICOU

When he is on the basketball court Andy Johnson, star forward for the Chicago Packers, is not a pleasant man. He is cruel and aflame although he's seemingly peaceful from the slight smile he wears on his face. Nothing is more important to him than winning, and if it means roughing the opposition a little more than usual, then he does it.

National Basketball Association players don't despise him—nor do the trainers who, at times, have to patch the bruises of their players as a result of Johnson's eagerness to win. "He and Bellamy are carrying the team," said one Packer fan recently. "He has kept the team alive," said another.

Off the field, dressed in an olive-green jacket with brown buttons, he looks like a young business man on a suburban weekend. The only clue to his roughneck personality is his six-foot, five-inch, 215 pound frame.

Johnson's contribution to the Packers is much more than his fiery spirit. He is averaging better than 13 points per game, performs magnificently on defense and is invariably involved in Packer's scoring sprees.

This season the Packers have been struggling to rise from the Western Division cellar and from the looks of things, they'll continue the struggle when the season ends.

ANDY JOHNSON

When Johnson was with Philadelphia last season he aided Wilt Chamberlain to a new NBA scoring championship. Prior to this season, last year was Johnson's best. He played in 79 games, scored 765 points for an 9.5 average, grabbed off 345 rebounds and passed off 207 assists.

However, last season's mark is only temporary because Andy is headed for bigger and better things.

Johnson's almost frightening competitive spirit was probably kindled during his younger days. While in the service, Johnson did some boxing. He made 37 appearances in the ring and won 35. Sid Flaherty, manager of Bobo Olsen, wanted Andy to turn professional. But Johnson's first love was basketball and it's a lucky thing for Packer coach Jim Pollard that Andy decided that basketball was a better way of life.

Johnson was a member of many College-All-Star teams during his college career at Portland College in California. Following a four year detour, he was signed by the Philadelphia organization but never got to play much appearing in only 67 games. The following year he did a little better playing in 75 games, scoring 615 points for a season's average of 8.2.

The Warriors passed Johnson to the Packers to help the new NBA entry make their debut in the professional ranks. But Johnson had a little trouble putting his point across to Pollard. It wasn't until this midseason's mark that Pollard got the message. Now Andy's position, at least for next year, is secure.

Coach Pollard recently issued the names of four members of the Packers who will not be up for grabs in next season's trades and Johnson was among the four.

Andy seems to improve with each game and has on several occasions, led the team with scoring honors. There seems to be no end to Johnson's capabilities. If he continues his present pace he will enter the elite group of top scorers in the NBA. But when he does, and the chances seem favorable, I hope he's still a member of the Packers.

The most critical damage to Dad and his career as a basketball player occurred when he was loaned to Chicago from the Philadelphia Warriors.

"Like a kid on the playground, Abe took his ball—me—and went home."—Andy Johnson

A sure sign of the end was when Saperstein, in his fury, decided to revitalize an amped-up version of the ABL, hoping it would surpass the success of the NBA. Abe felt like he'd given his all to the NBA. He'd loaned his top players and helped the league's expansion by creating the money-making doubleheaders with his Trotters. I can only imagine the slap in the face he must have felt when shortly afterward, his relationship ended with the NBA. Jerry Saperstein, his son, stated, "Abe was never the same after that incident."

JERRY SAPERSTEIN

July 23, 1992

Mr. Robert Criqui, Vice President Finance
The Pension Committee
National Basketball Association
645 Fifth Avenue
New York, New York 10022

Dear Mr. Criqui:

Andy Johnson was one of the finest professional basketball
players ever to compete in the game of basketball.

In 1962, I was associated with my father, Abe Saperstein, in the
operation of the American Basketball League and the legendary
Harlem Globetrotters Basketball Team in Chicago.

During that period, I spoke, on almost a daily basis, with Dave
Trager, then owner of the Chicago Zephyrs of the National
Basketball Association.

In the 1962-63 season, Andy Johnson was assigned and 'loaned'
to the Philadelphia Tapers of the ABL under his NBA contract.
NBA contracts in the late 1950's and early 1960's allowed for
players to be loaned to other professional teams with the lending
team retaining the rights to the player and his contract. As
long as the player was paid according to the terms of the contract,
the player had no choice as to where he played. This was not
only not unusual, but almost the norm.

After the Philadelphia Tapers suspended operations in 1963, Dave
Trager and the Chicago Zephyrs refused to honor their contract
with Andy Johnson and refused to place him on waivers to allow
any other NBA franchise to obtain his tremendous skills as a
professional basketball player.

It is hard to believe that this could happen; but it did and I
know it to be a fact.

Sincerely,

Jerry Saperstein

JS:se

A copy of a letter from Owner Abe's son Jerry, sent to the NBA on behalf of my father, while trying to obtain his pension.

In response, Saperstein convinced the National Alliance of Basketball Leagues (NABL) team owner Paul Cohen (Tuck Tapers) and the Amateur Athletic Union (AAU) owner George Steinbrenner (the current owner of the New York Yankees) to take the top NABL and AAU teams and players and form a rival league, a new ABL. Saperstein and Cohen each secretly made arrangements with local promoters in the other cities to finance those teams so there would be an eight-team league. Saperstein still wanted a team in LA to thwart the Lakers. So, he created the Los Angeles Jets in Los Angeles to take them on. He got Bill Sharman (former Celtic All-Star) as coach and signed former NBA players to give the team instant credibility. Ultimately, the idea backfired and the Jets did not last the season.

In Cleveland (Pipers), Steinbrenner's coach was the legendary John McClendon, who became the first African-American coach of a major pro basketball team. Steinbrenner signed All-American Jerry Lucas to a contract, planning to use the move to force his way into the NBA. It would have worked after winning the ABL title, but Abe sued to block the move and as a result, Steinbrenner had a team and no league. Instead of returning to the ABL, Steinbrenner dismantled the team.

Paul Cohen, who quietly owned the Pittsburgh team as well as officially owning the Tapers, moved the Tapers again from New York, where they had been one of the NABL's strongest teams for years, to Philadelphia, where he hoped to fill the void of the Warriors' shocking move to San Francisco. Remember, the Warriors were originally in the ABL and won the first ABL Championship and with the Warriors' move (hence the Golden State Warriors), for the first time, Philadelphia had no professional team in the 1962-63 season.

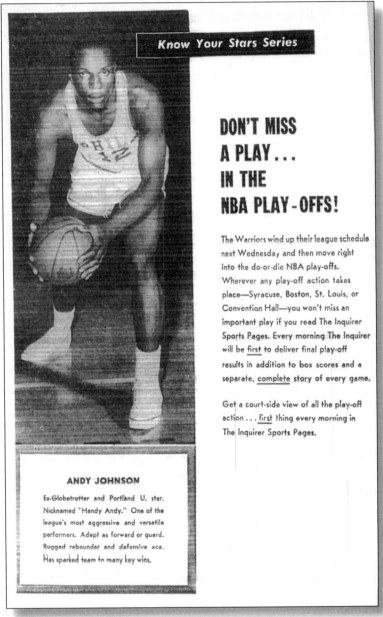

Andy Johnson. Full page advertisment in one of the top Philadelphia newspapers (The Inquirer).

Unfortunately with no new money to fund the league and a poor turnout on New Year's Eve of 1962, the league folded and Saperstein and Cohen decided to throw in the towel. Just like that, the league that pioneered the three-point shot and the wider foul line (both eventually adopted by the rest of the basketball world) disappeared.

After playing for the Packers, unable to be picked up by any other team, and still the property of Abe, Dad went to play for the Philadelphia Tapers along with other greats like Sylvester "Sly" Blye and the legendary Cleo Hill. The Tapers and the Pittsburg Rens had a great rivalry, especially when the Rens acquired a young star in Connie Hawkins. But, because of all the circumstances surrounding the ABL, the Tapers were short-lived and Philadelphia didn't see another professional basketball team until the Syracuse Nationals were sold to Irv Kosloff and Ike Richman and became the Philadelphia Sixers.

The history is important, because some of the negative back-door dealings associated with it were responsible for destroy-ing a man's livelihood. It is more about the principle than the money. When you put a man through what they did to Andy Johnson, it is reasonable to honor the one year that made the difference so he could receive his pension.

Fortunately, I was able to find Dad's thirty-year-old contract and had the help of the son of the man who, no matter what we might think of his methods, gave professional basketball signifi-cance. Jerry Saperstein sent a letter verifying the fact that loan-ing did occur in the fifties and sixties—and it was that letter that finally forced the NBA to honor Dad's pension.

In talking with Jerry, he reminded me that Abe was very upset over the entire situation and unfortunately died a few

Jack Kiser   MAR 15 63 DN

After 14 Years, a Place for Andy

For 14 years now Andy Johnson has been searching for his place in basketball. The eager hunt has carried him from Portland to Paris, Mexico City, London, Moscow, Buenos Aires, Philadelphia, Chicago and a few hundred other towns.

During the early years Andy Johnson lived on hope and peanut butter and jelly sandwiches, first at Portland U. and then with the Globetrotters. Then came the big break: the big time. A modest contract with the Philadelphia Warriors. Ever since Andy Johnson has been living on bitter disappointments, frustrations and peanut butter and jelly sandwiches.

Andy Johnson stands 6-5, weighs 255, and other basketball players will tell you honestly that he's good enough to play on any pro team in the country. His muscles have muscles and every one is well coordinated. He can play the pivot like a Houdini, and he can go outside and bomb with a quick flip of a one-hander (he once scored 72 points against the College All-Stars without taking a shot from less than 25 feet out). He'll bang with anybody for rebounds and he never loafs on defense.

"He's tough and he's good," says all-time great Paul Arizin, "He has to help any team he plays with."

'Not Big Leagues, But Nice'

Despite these credentials, Andy Johnson doesn't play in the big time any more. He plays for Allentown in the Eastern League, which isn't exactly ready to challenge the NBA in a nose-to-nose showdown. But Andy isn't complaining. He's playing with a first-place team. He's playing regular and he's being paid regular and he's being treated regular. And, as Andy puts it, "You can't ask for anything more."

"No, it's not the big leagues, but it's nice," Andy says. "The people up there like Dave Walters (the club president) and Brendon McCann (the coach) have been real good to me. I think I'm helping the team and I wouldn't mind playing for them the rest of my life. Just get a job here in Philly and play for Allentown and know where you stand all the time. That if you do the job you have a job."

Andy (and many others) figured he was doing a job with the Warriors. He played for them three years and was a solid starter and one of the league's most respected defensemen in 1960-61. But the next year found him in Chicago, dumped into the player pot of Eddie Gottlieb and grabbed eagerly by the new Packers.

Andy did a job with the Packers, too. Only two other teammates outscored him and one of them had 300 more minutes playing time. "I didn't get much of a chance at first," Andy recalls, "but I didn't complain. I figured the coach (Jim Pollard) was trying to do his job the best he knew how. But then I started to play regular and I averaged 29.23 points, 11 rebounds and six assists of the season.

"Our last game with Los Angeles shakes my hand and tells me how and how I've improved, and my place in basketball."

Came this season and Chicago (Zephyrs) and a new coach was right back where he started. "I went to camp a starter and they treated me like a regular scrimmages I'd always score found myself sitting down and oh,' I told myself, 'Here we go scrimmage for the press and points and got some big write

shoulders sadly and headed for the Eastern League. He hooked on with Allentown for $75 per game. The Jets were three games back of Camden when he joined them and they're a half-game out front now. Coach McCann says Andy is the big reason for the reversal, so he'd be a bargain at twice the price.

Does he ever dream of getting back into the NBA?

"Well, I'm 29 years old now (he's really 31, but everybody fudges a bit on their age when they reach the 30-plateau) and I know there's not much chance of getting a solid no-cut contract. That's the only way I'd go back.

"Basketball is my life. I worked hard to get where I was, and I got shoved back. I don't like to get shoved because I fight when I do. And I don't like to fight, so I don't want to get shoved any more. Things are nice at Allentown. No shoving or anything like that. Nice and peaceful, you know. The kind of people you like to play for."

After 14 years it seems as if Andy Johnson finally has found a place in basketball.

JOHNSON

> Andy (and many others) figured he was doing a job with the Warriors. He played for them three years and was a solid starter and one of the league's most respected defensemen in 1960-61. But the next year found him in Chicago, dumped into the player pot of Eddie Gottlieb and grabbed eagerly by the new Packers.

Zephyr Release a Mystery

"I couldn't believe it, so I ask him why. 'Well,' he tells me, 'I just can't see how you scored that many points last year. We just can't use you.' Well I had to have a better reason than that, so I went to Dave Trager (the club president).

"Trager tells me there wasn't anything personal involved. That the coach said I was a perfect gentleman, but I just didn't know the plays. That was the silliest thing I ever heard. All McMahon was running was the old St. Louis plays and I'd been playing defense against Pettit and Hagan for four years. But it was his club and his decision and there was nothing I could do about it."

So Andy sat back and waited for some other club to claim him. None did. Some observers say it was because the league had become over-saturated with Negro players and the owners had decided to reduce the number.

Some writers tried to prod Andy into blasting the league, but he wouldn't go for the racial angle bit. "I just want to live and let live," he explains. "I'm no troublemaker, but I know there was some funny stuff going on."

So Andy packed his bags and joined the ill-fated Philadelphia Tapers. When the ABL folded he shrugged his years later, in March 1966. How ironic it is that the contract Dad signed, which the NBA claimed they wouldn't honor, was the same contract I found filed away in the NBA's own office in 1996. That signed contract substantiated Dad's fifth year under contract, after they'd turned him down multiple times. When I showed up with the old and tattered contract, the NBA pension committee's mouths dropped to the floor—and still, they hesitated.

"Make me understand why I was the only one. The only one they would not put on waivers so that I could have been picked up by someone else."—Andy Johnson

To this day, many players and coaches that I've talked with wanted to know what happened with Dad's contract with the NBA after Chicago's move to Baltimore (the team became the Baltimore Bullets, then the Washington Bullets and now, the Washington Wizards). Why wasn't a waiver instituted on his behalf so he could return to the league? The answers to those questions most likely lie in the graves of the gatekeepers of the information during that time.

TRICK 'n TREAT

Stick, famous French cartoonist, intrigued with tales of the ball-handling magic of the Harlem Globetrotters, decided to catch their hilarity, and this page of sketches is an "on-the-scene" report direct from Paris.

11

It Takes More Than Love

A DEFUNCT TAPER TEAM, A LOST CONTRACT, and no waivers. Andy Johnson was in the middle of an owners' dispute and he had to do something fast. He loved the game of basketball—that is all he really knew—but Dad had a family of five kids at the time, with me on the way. It was 1963.

At this point, his lack of education haunted him. He was a Louisiana transplant in sunny California who was placed on a straight course of basketball by his teachers, coaches, and owners, while others went to school to study science and English. Dad understood the impact of his limited education. He felt like basketball wasn't just his only option, but it was the only option that chose him. I often asked him why he didn't get a lawyer. He remembered the last time he tried to get a lawyer. Plus, a lawyer cost money and there wasn't any money coming in. Dad felt trapped and had to put food on the table. He told me:

"I had to figure out how to make it. Some nights I would go on the floor thinking about how I was going to pay our rent. By the Grace of God, He let me survive."— Andy Johnson

This statement brought tears to my eyes.

Dad did what he could for his family and went to work where a lot of great players played. It was the Eastern Basketball League (EBL), established in 1947, the oldest North American basketball league. After a name change in 1978, the Eastern League became the Continental Basketball League (CBA).

At that time, the CBA was the only league that allowed blacks to play. Those black players that got drafted by the NBA like Julius McCoy and Wally Choice, who were turned away from the NBA door. Or a person like Carl Green who chose to walk away from the Warriors (NBA) when the team wanted to pay him less and change his position. This is where they could continue to show off their tremendous talent. I remember looking at a box score from a game between Williamsport 143 that had players like Choice and Green over Easton 142 (Hal Lear). I would have loved to see that game.

The CBA was often called the forgotten league, in spite of its instrumental role in the development of the NBA. The NBA would also take players from this league. There were a few Philadelphia favorites that made an impact in the EBL/CBA: Sonny Hill; Roman Turman; Jay Norman; Walt Simon; and even the legendary coach of Temple University, John Cheney. When there wasn't a professional team in Philadelphia, greats like Tom Gola and Paul Arizin also played in this league.

The EBL is where College All-Americans, Original Harlem Globetrotters, NBA greats, and neighborhood basketball stars were able to play together and against each other. The EBL/CBA was extremely competitive, and so with no more legal or contractual ties to the NBA, Dad was recruited by the Allentown Jets.

While playing for the Jets, Andy Johnson led them to several championships. One reporter called him the most complete player he had ever seen. Dad played every position. In addition to that, he was an excellent defender, something that is rare even by today's standards. In one game, he held his old friend and teammate (one of the NBA 50 greatest) Paul Arizin to only three field goals during the championship and on many occasions he garnered All-League honors.

Andy played with the Jets for another seven years while he still waited to possibly clear up his standing with the NBA and get a waiver. Unfortunately, his playing for the Allentown Jets wound up being the death of his NBA career.

Dad periodically went back to play for the Globetrotters, but it was never the same as it was during the heyday of the fifties. The foolery that had been incorporated into the Globetrotter games as a *supplement* to the phenomenal basketball aptitude of the players had become the central focus and purpose of the organization. Before, the serious ball players could run the score up on a team and then bring in people like Meadowlark Lemon and Tex Harrison to entertain the crowd. Now they were at the forefront and were the face of the Trotters, being clowns and taking away the true reason why the Trotters were formed. This is one of the reasons why people today think that the Trotters were not serious ball players. The NBA was integrating and getting serious, while the commercialization of the Trotters forced the

Top Row: Andy Johnson, Carl Green, Hank Whitney (Iowa State), Tom Stith (All-American, St. Bonaventure). Bottom Row: Walt Simon (Kentucky ABA), John Nacincik, Johnny Jones

players to become all hands and smiles with no depth, particularly when the team was sold to the Metromedia Corporation.

Some of the Trotters were unhappy with these changes and wanted to form a union. The plan was for the team to go on strike and for the players not to show up at camp. But that did not happen. Many of the main players showed up anyway, which left the other players out in the cold, which was a definite indicator that the once brotherly climate of the team had changed.

Dad was told to report to camp immediately or he would be in the same situation as some of his counterparts, so for him, playing for this newer version of his beloved Trotters became just another paycheck. And, of course, the NBA never came calling, either. Dad was blackballed by the league because of his association with Abe.

CURLY NEIL AND MEADOWLARK LEMON
When the Harlem Globetrotters appeared on television, they became commercialized and people did not take them as serious basketball players.

For Dad, playing in the Eastern League was nice. In fact, after all of the drama that danced around him upon his sudden departure from the "big" leagues, Dad was tired. He wanted a place that allowed him to play *his* game, and the Allentown Jets in the Eastern Basketball League was that place. He scored, he assisted, and in addition to allowing others to stand out, he was able to shine as the team's captain. Dad was quoted in one magazine article as saying, "Basketball is my life. I worked hard to get where I was and I got shoved back. I don't like to get shoved because I fight when I do, and I don't like to fight, so I don't want to get shoved anymore. Things are nice at Allentown. No shoving or anything like that. Nice and peaceful, you know, the kind of people you like to play for."

***

I could pretend that my father was the perfect man and present an idealistic view of him, but then I wouldn't be telling the truth and, if anything, that's what his story and his life were about—the truth. Dad lived his life being true to the man he was, in spite of any faults.

With Mom, I came to understand why they were together, but also why they ended up apart, despite the great love they had for each other. The mismanagement and not having enough money was a recurring issue for them. And, remember, for all of his gentlemanly qualities, my father was rough around the edges. He wasn't a guy who made his bed every day or who neatly folded his socks and underwear. I'm sure this was partially a byproduct of living his life on the road, traveling from hotel to hotel.

My mother, on the other hand, was a neat freak. The curtains had to match the bedspread and the bedspread had to match the carpet; that was the type of woman she was. However, when dad would come home, he'd throw his clothes all over the place, and those little things built up over time, wearing on her over the course of their marriage.

Also, although it was never confirmed, I believe that neither of my parents were faithful to each other, particularly my father. There were never any illegitimate children, but I think some affairs occurred while my dad was on the road. As I've alluded to before, he was a Globetrotter and later an NBA player. He was loved superficially by many in more ways than one. He also had a flirtatious nature that attracted women of every kind, and while I know he loved my mother and our family, I know he wasn't always the most subtle man, either. In fact, my father told me a story about when the Globetrotters met the King and Queen of England and he actually winked at the queen. The other players were shocked and told him that he couldn't wink at the Queen. My father, in Andy Johnson fashion, answered, "Should I have winked at the King?"

My father had a charm about him that, in hindsight, was probably effective in getting the attention of women he met on the road. As wrong as that is—and it's definitely wrong—the one thing I can say is that, to my knowledge, none of his activities were ever brought to our home. However, I suppose my mother could only pretend not to know for so long.

And, sometimes my father stayed on the road longer than necessary to avoid hearing my mother's fairly constant complaints about how he was being treated by the administration. Probably, to some degree, he stayed away because he didn't want to be reminded of the truth in her words.

Dad used to say, "I'll fly now and pay later." It was his way of trying to get away. Was that right? No, of course it wasn't. As a child, I certainly would have liked my dad home more; but Dad did pay attention to his children when he was home. When Dad came home from the road, he'd sit down with us and talk for hours and hours, and that almost made up for how long he was gone. I think he felt like he could impart his philosophies to us that way, despite what was going on internally in our home.

Andy Johnson, Allentown Jets

12

My Dad, A Man of Character

WHEN THEY WERE ABLE TO, Mom and Dad traveled quite a bit. And, being the youngest child, I was a major beneficiary. When Mom went to Dad's games she would usually take me with her, so I saw things that most kids my age and in my neighborhood never got a chance to see. Wherever he had a game, from New York to Puerto Rico, if Mom went, I tagged along. For the games we couldn't attend, I remember tracking Dad on the map. I would say, "Okay, he's in South Carolina today and tomorrow he'll be in Atlanta." And whenever I got mail from him, I'd be keyed up and excited.

Some nights when Dad was expected home, I'd beg my mom for permission to wait up for him. Despite the fact that my eyes would be heavy with sleep's approach, I refused to let the sandman win the battle because I was determined to attack my dad with hugs as soon as he walked through the door. He'd come in and, being the silly guy that he was, he'd do something crazy. We'd wrestle or he'd have a funny gift for me. That's the side of him to which few people were privy. Most people saw him as Andy "Enforcer" Johnson—but to me, he was just my dad.

It was tough. I really didn't have my father until later on in my life. When Dad traveled, I didn't have ready access to him. I couldn't email, text, or call him on his cell phone, and maybe that's why I didn't take him for granted. We made the most of the time we had together.

The fact is, I had a father figure growing up, but I didn't have a lot of the father-and-son interaction that I wanted at the time. Dad didn't take me to my basketball games or help me with my science fair projects. We maintained our relationship via phone calls or letters and postcards. Dad would provide me my own mini-mental vacation by sending me postcards, stamps, and coins from the various countries he visited. I was fascinated by the exotic places that I'd learn about, so I was able to make his absences okay for me. If I talked to my dad once every other week or once a month, I looked forward to that. The calls and correspondence were significant for me and were what I grew to expect from him. Sometimes if he was playing somewhere close, like in New York, my mom and I would drive up to see him. Sometimes he'd come home in the middle of the night and surprise me with a small gift.

I missed him, though. When he went on overseas tours with the Trotters for long periods of time, I used to tell him every chance I got that I missed him and he'd always say to me, "Every time I spend a dollar, I'm going to think of you, Mark."

For a long time, I never understood what he meant. I kept asking him what he meant by that and he wouldn't tell me. Finally, after three or four months away on the road, he came home and he told me, "Remember I said that every time I spent a dollar, I was going to think of you?" Then he reached behind his back and pulled out a long sweat sock filled with change and he gave it to me. He told me to do whatever I wanted with it, but to never forget to save some for a rainy day. It meant so much to me, because I knew that whenever he broke a dollar on the road, he was thinking of his little Mark back home in Philly.

Needless to say, I became a "big dog" on my block. I could buy all of the Lemonhead, Boston Baked Beans, and any other candy I wanted. In that gesture I saw, given his situation, how much my dad loved me in spite of not being as physically available as I or he would have liked, and I think that sense of worth and devotion is the most powerful emotion a little boy could ever experience. Knowing he cared for me was immensely important.

In order to maintain a family of six kids and a wife and a home, Dad would send all of his salary home and live off his per diem on the road (which was not much). An article I read stated that the Trotters made a whole lot more than was advertised, but of course that was not the case.

As I grew up, I realized it wasn't about the money for him. I really couldn't get upset because my father didn't give me something I wanted, as many kids do in this day and age. I was just happy to have this special relationship with him being on the road so much. Although I won't deny that it was definitely a trade-off.

I had a special connection with my dad that kept me on a straight path, even if it was through just a phone call. That's why I believe it's important for women who may not have their children's father in the home to still put him on some kind of pedestal in the eyes of their children. Even if he's not living in the home, sometimes having the dad as an absent authority figure can be helpful in disciplining children.

My mom used to say, "Don't make me call your father!" and that was all I needed to hear. I remember one time I'd messed up really badly and I was on the phone with my dad. He said, "If I have to come home for you, boy, you're going to get it!" I told him, "Well, you never have to come home then, Dad." Not that I didn't want him home, but I didn't want him to come home just to discipline me. Later on I found out that Mom and Dad had many laughs about that incident.

Dad had his way of disciplining us without physical abuse, of which I am glad, considering how big he was. He was effective. My older brother Andy, Jr., told me a story about when he was sixteen years old and drank some beer after one of his games, before he came home. He thought he could get by Dad without him smelling the alcohol on his breath and he thought he did, since Dad didn't say anything to him that night. When he arrived home from school the next day, though, Dad followed him into his room with a bottle of hard liquor and two cups. Dad said, "If you are going to drink, you're going to drink with me." Needless to say, there weren't any drinks poured that day, but that was Dad's way of saying, "I know what you did" and my brother felt ashamed.

Andy Johnson was everybody's dad. My friends, especially the ones who didn't have their fathers around growing up or who'd lost a close relationship with their fathers as they became adults, would gravitate to him for advice and encouragement.

And for me—well, there was nothing like having lunch with my father as an adult. I could call and talk to him and my friends could, too. People loved talking with him because his wisdom always seemed to be of astronomical proportions. He was my dad, but he was an authority father figure for many people, as I found out when he died.

As an adult, my relationship with Dad developed to the point where he would always be there. There was a point in my adult life when I came to my own crossroads and I could have gone down the wrong path and ended up not living the life that I was called or raised to live. However, my dad was there for me, at that pivotal point, to guide me through my trials.

He used to say, "You get what you need, when you need it." While he may not have thought of that in the context of the part he would play in my life, it was true. I got my dad when I needed him the most—and that was all that ever mattered.

From his perspective, though, I think that whenever he saw me with my son, dropping him off and taking him places, Dad realized that he had missed a huge part of my life—of all of his children's lives. I never wanted him to regret that, but because I know that his love for us was so strong, I'm sure he did.

My father was gone ten months out of the year, traveling with the Trotters and then playing in the NBA and the Eastern League. The other two months, he worked various jobs, playing the provider role superbly. I didn't have a whole lot of time with him, which made the time we did share important. When I got my chance, I made the most of my time with him, instead of being bitter over what I may not have gotten as a child.

That's why I believe it is important for fathers to maintain a relationship with their children, even if they don't live with them. I know firsthand the anxiety and excitement a child goes through when not seeing his father for long periods of time. The undeniable connection between fathers and sons extends beyond the lines of households and it must be maintained at all costs. Whether it was a phone call or a letter, I feared and loved my dad, even if he wasn't always around.

Unfortunately, times have changed from when I was growing up. Nowadays young people have many more distractions and the perspective of parenting has changed tremendously. Dad used to say, "Love is not an emotion. It's an act." How powerful is that?

Many parents I met in the youth program I worked for would say, in reference to a wayward child, "He's eighteen now, so he can get out of my house." They didn't realize that parenting doesn't stop at a certain age.

Both my mother and father parented me until the day they died; as a result, I showed them the respect they deserved for just as long. The dynamics may have changed, my ability to choose for myself may have amended their control a little bit from childhood to adulthood, but they never stopped parenting me. Children have too many options in today's world, and by being a consistent parent, you can influence those options and choices significantly. Children don't raise themselves as much as we might wish that they did.

Khalil Gibran, a prophet my dad greatly admired said, "Children don't come from us, they come through us." Dad believed that wholeheartedly.

We can't stop influencing our children's lives just because they've reached some government designation of adulthood, especially when they reach out for our help.

***

Andy Johnson had a way of telling a story. His double-meaning storytelling was compounded by an unbelievable sense of humor. Statements like: "My father was Jack Johnson and I took Doris Day to the prom" were not funny, but Dad's way of saying he was not only related to one of toughest men and was with the top actress of the era. Who can top that combination? That is how much confidence he had in himself.

Yes, Andy Johnson was an ingenious storyteller. He was my own personal, paternal griot. There was hardly ever a time when he was not engaged in conversation. The way he'd weave a tale or express an experience seemed poetic and yet always genuine. Through his stories, I was able to uncover the man behind the entity I knew as my father. His stories allowed our relationship to blossom from father/son to best friends, and it was in these stories that my dad's greatest pains were revealed. I guess it would be clichéd to say that growing up as a black boy in the forties and fifties was difficult, but then again, even the truth can be subject to interpretation.

***

Dad was a giver. If you look at any of the pictures of him playing basketball, he was always giving. I don't know if it was the way he was raised—the fact that he never became attached to things.

Dad never judged people. Instead he tried to learn from everyone he met. As I mentioned before, when the Trotters played in other countries, Dad never wanted to stay in the city or the touristy areas. He wanted to go see the people. He ventured into the villages and the parts of cities that were not well-known so he could see how the citizens lived and to learn their philosophies. He wanted to communicate with the average, everyday people because despite being a basketball star, that's how he viewed himself. At home, he would always take the time to talk with young people and to sign autographs. He believed that he owed it to the public to be a gentleman at all times. Dad felt like he owed the public good character and a standard of excellence in every area of his life.

This maxim was never more evident than when Dad stopped playing professional basketball. He never told anyone of his past. Many years after he'd stopped playing, Dad would work at various jobs and his bosses would never know who he was or what he'd accomplished in his life, and he never felt the need to tell them.

I'll never forget the time I showed one of Dad's former employers a tape that talked about Andy Johnson and other Globetrotter and NBA players who paved the way for the Michael Jordans and Magic Johnsons of the world. Her mouth hung open in astonishment. She had no idea. And it wasn't some weird self-sacrifice or pride that kept Dad from talking about what he had done. He was well aware of who he was and what he did for basketball, but he didn't see any need to flaunt his past in the present, especially if it held no impact on his future. He lived in the moment until the day he died.

"I don't need anyone to validate me."—Andy Johnson

In addition to having a generous personality, Dad was a hard worker. He was as diligent as they come. It amazed me how Dad could play a season of professional basketball and then work as a bricklayer in the summertime for John B. Kelly, the man who is often called the architect of Philadelphia (as well as a part of the family that birthed Princess Grace Kelly). In fact, I have a hard time imagining any of today's professional ball players working as a laborer for a construction company. But this was a requirement for my dad and many of the other guys who played professional basketball in that era. They couldn't afford to live on the basketball salaries alone. And, knowing Dad, he would have worked even if he didn't have to. And since he had to, his outlook was eternal optimism. He didn't view his summer gig as work. He used to tell us that he was keeping in shape for the season. Once again, Andy turned lemons into lemonade.

Dad participated in charity events where he gave of his time and energy without the expectation of payment. In addition to supporting many local leagues, he formed the Andy Johnson Basketball Academy, to teach fundamental basketball skills to inner-city students in Philadelphia and Southern New Jersey while also providing encouragement and support for their academic pursuits. He adamantly stressed that students who weren't doing well in school weren't allowed to play basketball and had to spend that time studying. Many young people who'd been saved from the streets or from having their athletic prowess exploited were devastated when they learned Dad had passed.

"They let me coach at the jail, but not on the outside."— Andy Johnson

While still playing with the Eastern League, Dad became the athletic director at Eastern State Correctional Institution, where he faced his biggest challenge yet. Eastern State was a penitentiary for hardened criminals, as well as those who were deemed criminally insane. These were the guys who weren't allowed in a regular prison. It was also where the infamous gangster Al Capone was housed.

Andy had dealt with tough guys on the court, and even ones that were on the run from the law a time or two, but now he had to form a team with hardened criminals who exhibited their hostility in all areas of their lives. And he had to teach them how to play effectively against teams like St. Joseph's College and the Philadelphia Court Jesters (a semi-pro team in the 1960s and 70s.)

One way Dad's prison team would guarantee a sure advantage in games was during the introduction of the lineup. While St. Joseph's announced their team members as "six-foot nine and a freshman out of Ben Franklin High school," Dad's team was introduced as "six-foot nine and doing eighty years for double homicide." The St. Joseph's team would start the game shaking in their shorts.

Andy's goal was to teach these men what he'd always taught me: basketball was a game of life and that the rules of the game were the same as the rules of life. Since they'd decided long ago to live by no rules but their own, dad faced a true challenge. Yet he passed with flying colors. He treated the men with respect and therefore he garnered their respect in return. In fact, because Dad oversaw all of the sports activities, he would actually appoint an inmate as "commissioner" over each sport, such as basketball, football, etc. The commissioner would appoint coaches and the coaches would go to the yard and get their players. The players would then sign contracts and begin practice. These commissioners were also able to suspend players for breaking the rules. Dad was an observer and he took his cue

Basketball Star Heads Program

Prison Sports Score High

By REM RIEDER
Of The Inquirer Staff

Andy Johnson has played basketball under all types of circumstances. He was a topflight forward for the old Philadelphia Warriors. He played for Portland University, the Harlem Globetrotters and in the weekend Eastern League and in more schoolyards than he can count.

But as wise as he is in the ways of the court, Andy Johnson is encountering new personnel problems in his latest position.

"We had a guy who was 6-6 who could make any pro team," Andy Johnson was saying. "He was good when he got here and he really developed while he was here. But then something happened and he was transferred to Holmesburg."

TRANSFERS HURT

Andy Johnson is athletic director at Eastern State Correctional Institution, the old stone fortress at 21st st. and Fairmount ave.

He finds it tough sometimes to have his varsity at full strength for visiting teams like the St. Joseph's College varsity and the Philadelphia Court Jesters. Things like transfers and releases can get in the way.

At 32, Johnson is still active with Allentown in the Eastern League. But his prison program is not limited to basketball. The inmates also play football (tackle, of course), softball, volleyball and soccer.

In each sport, Johnson gives the inmates a major roll in or-

ANDY JOHNSON

and get their players. They even give them contracts. And the commissioner can suspend players if they break the rules."

The suspensions play an important part in keeping the players, not known for their respect for authority, in line.

"Sports are a big thing to most of them," Johnson said. "If they can't play, they just sit around. And if they want to play, they follow the rules."

LEARN TO ADJUST

And it is here, Johnson thinks, that the importance of his sports program lies.

"Through sports, they learn that they can abide by the rules," he said. "Once they learn to adjust to the rulebook in sports, it's not too hard f...

Aided by F

some of them to adjust   *sic*

"After all, most of them a here for breaking the rules

Right now it's football se son at Eastern State and ever body gets up for the games ea Sunday. As a visitor left tl prison recently he was told l a guard to come back for th Sunday's showdown between tl Spartans and the Bulldogs.

"This has got to be a goc one," the guard said.

To play football at Easter State it helps to be a little b tough. The out-of bounds mark on one side of the field is stone wall.

The visitor said to Andy Joh son that a ball-carrier would l wise to stay away from the wa side of the field.

"Yeh, but it you try to tack someone over there, you bett hit him," Johnson pointed ou "If you miss you hit the wa yourself."

INMATE HELPS OUT

As he tends to his duties Joh son is often accompanied by h "assistant," an inmate name George Miketish.

"He's my right-hand man," Johnson said. "He's always wit me and it makes things a k easier. Sometimes I'll let hi do things like appoint the leagu commissioner."

Johnson, in turn, has receive the high esteem of the warde Joseph Brierley. "He's real done a great job," Brierley sai "He's gotten them very inte ested in his program."

Andy Johnson has bee athletic director at Easter State almost three years. Th job combines his lifelong inter est in sports with the opportu nity to help other people, and he sure he'll stay in the field.

LEARN TO ADJUST

And it is here, Johnson thinks, that the importance of his sports program lies.

"Through sports, they learn that they can abide by the rules," he said. "Once they learn to adjust to the rulebook in sports, it's not too hard for some of them to adjust   *sic*

Andy ran the sports program at the famous Eastern State Penitentiary.

Andy teaching kids overseas in the early 1950s while traveling with the Trotters.

from his years playing under Abe Saperstein on how to manage a basketball team effectively.

Dad viewed the inmates as men, not just numbers in a jumpsuit. He allowed them to take responsibility for their actions, sometimes for the first time in their lives, and to be accountable for the rules of the game. That's how he lived his life and he expected that if they ever were released, they'd do the same.

"Basketball is the game of life and GOD is the referee."—Andy Johnson

13

Reality Strikes Back

DAD ALWAYS SAID THAT THE WAY HE WAS TREATED by North Hollywood, Portland University, and the leagues didn't bother him, but I know it did. And I believe the sting burned him more during his last days here. It's one thing to pontificate and argue about what they did to him, it's another to actually see it in black and white and to see what should have been done—and wasn't—to protect and care for him as an athlete and as a person.

Dad felt the wrongness when he saw the Portland transcript and that thirty-year-old NBA contract. He knew there was something not right about the negotiations regarding *his* career. He knew he had been taken advantage of, even though he had a clear understanding of the world he lived in. At the time, since whatever was happening always seemed to take him to another level, he never allowed the full reality of the slavery aspect sink in too deeply. But when I showed him that transcript and he realized how pivotal it was in his life, particularly its effects on his efforts to get a coaching job or accomplish some of his other goals, I know it hurt him in an unimaginable way.

After I received my college diploma, Dad watched in silent admiration as my degree helped me obtain a positive position in life. Many times he was asked whether he had a degree or not and because he didn't, he missed out on significant opportunities. What I don't think he ever realized is that when I walked across that stage and picked up that diploma, I did it for the both of us.

"I understand why some slaves took their lives in their hands in order to read a book. By not giving me an education or allowing me to learn in school they took the things I would have loved to do like coaching and teaching. They took some of my brain power away by letting me go through school without going to class."—Andy Johnson

The realization that he'd physically and emotionally given so much of himself to North Hollywood and Portland, and that they had turned him and his skills into a commodity that ultimately would be discarded without payment, was a powerful eye-opener. Yes, these people gave him temporary rewards for his athletic achievements, like cars and material things, but those couldn't be carried into his future. So, even though Dad said he wasn't angry, his actions would prove otherwise.

Dad would turn down invitations to various reunions or celebrations that were held for him later on in his life. I believe this was his way of holding onto a deep-rooted bitterness about not being allowed to play *his* game and being able to show the world for only a short period who he was as a basketball player.

It was his way of dealing with never being allowed to fully complete his career, his basketball life-cycle, whether that led to coaching or broadcasting.

Fortunately, he was finally able to get the honor due him in a way that was much more important than any national recognition could offer. I held an intimate party at my house a year before he died which, to his surprise, was his own special induction into his home hall of fame. Although it was catered, his "induction" was more like a big barbeque with all of those close to him at various times in his life in attendance. I invited his friends from North Hollywood, the Trotters, Warriors, the Army, etc.

You see, Dad was real. He was a relaxed person and didn't care for the black-tie affairs. Remember, he grew up in the South and spent most of his early childhood barefoot, so that simplicity resonated even in his later years. I knew he'd want to be around real people and he enjoyed this type of "induction" more than some big event that honored Andy Johnson, the ballplayer, with half of the people in attendance not really knowing him and everything that truly made him great. One of my most powerful memories of that barbeque was when he leaned over and whispered in my ear, *"You made me famous, again."* I knew he was happy and proud.

One might say that to make the comparison of slaves working in the fields and getting lynched to the mistreatment of blacks in the game of basketball is extreme. I must remind anyone with those thoughts, though, to think of the definition of slavery. Slavery is more than just hangings and beatings. As stated earlier, slavery is defined as the state of being under the control of another person and/or work done under unacceptable conditions for little or no pay.

My dad (and others) worked hard and showed off his talents; everybody got rich but him. Actually it isn't the money so much. I am more upset that his education was stolen. And, to top it off, Dad was not allowed to continue on the track that was made available to him because he was black. Doors were shut because of greed and racial injustice.

All current and past athletes, in any sport, need to recognize and understand that people like my father paved the way for them to have the freedom to reach the end of the line. People like Joe Lapchick (Original Celtics), who participated in the first jump ball between a white man and a black man (Tarzan Cooper with the Harlem Rens) in professional basketball. Mr. Lapchick had the courage to help bring blacks into the league and was responsible for signing one of the first African Americans, Nat "Sweetwater" Clifton, to the New York Knicks.

I also think of John Wooden and Red Auerbach. These men have been responsible for the success of many blacks in basketball. There was no way you were going to play for Mr. Wooden and not get an education. He knew getting an education was the only way his players would have a better chance at a productive life. Mr. Wooden knew one day basketball would be over for all of his players. He did not make selfish decisions when it came to someone else's life. The great Red Auerbach, who broke all the rules when it came to racial barriers in the NBA, looked beyond the prejudices and simply wanted to win. He recognized that basketball is a team sport and your opponent can be black or white.

During one game in Boston Gardens, a teammate turned to Dad and said, "Well, Andy. We finally made it to the big times." Dad immediately pointed up to Red Auerbach who was smoking a cigar and said, "When we are sitting back, watching the games, and smoking cigars like Red, then we will have made it!"

ALLENTOWN

Jets

EASTERN PROFESSIONAL BASKETBALL LEAGUE

ROCKNE HALL   FOURTH AND CHEW STREETS   ALLENTOWN, PA.

JOHN T. GRANER, President • WILLIAM J. MONTZMAN, General Manager

FRANK PFEIFFER, JR., Vice-President • JOHN NACINCIK, Coach

ANDY JOHNSON: "WE OWE IT TO THE PUBLIC"

. . . . . By Johnny Kimock

Before the NBA all-star game two years ago, a terrific snowstorm hit Boston, but it was nothing compared to the uproar caused by Bill Russell's article, "I Owe The Public Nothing," which came out about the same time.

Russell said some powerful things in his story. He criticized the public's attitude towards Negro players in the National Basketball Association. And he criticized what he called a quota which limits their numbers on each team.

"If Bill really believes he owes the public nothing, then I, as a fellow Negro, must disagree," said Allentown's Andy Johnson. "We Negroes, and the white players, too, owe them something. We owe them a good game. After the game, we owe them a certain amount of courtesy."

If anyone had predicted eight years ago that a Majority of all-star players in the NBA and in the Eastern League would be Negroes, he would have caused some disagreement even with members of the Negro race. But this season, 13 of the 20 all-stars in the NBA were Negroes. In the Eastern League, of the 18 all-stars are Negroes - 6 in the Eastern Division and 7 in the Western Division.

Johnson went on to say, "The greatest of these and the greatest player I have ever seen or played against, is Bill Russell. Yet I don't think Bill speaks entirely for me or for all the Negroes in professional basketball. Let me explain what I mean by courtesies to the public. I like a cigarette to relax me after a game. And occasionally a beer is fine, too. But I seldom smoke or drink in public where a youngster is liable to see me. To me, this is a courtesy. We are their idols. They come to see us play. The least we can do is retain the image they have of us.

"When I played at Portland University," Andy said, "I was one of the first Negro athletes in the history of the school. All of the sports writers were on my side. They really were great—100 percent for me. And I've never had any trouble with writers in

the NBA. My years at Portland were among the greatest in my life. In my final game, I fouled out. They gave me a standing ovation. And my coach, Jim Torson, had tears in his eyes when he hugged me and said: 'this is it, Andy—you just don't forget moments like that'."

With his head bowed, Andy continued, "I grew up in the suburb of North Hollywood, California and I attended North Hollywood High School. On the

When the Negro began his push for equality, he was starting from the back. The rear of the bus you might say. He finally got to the front of the bus and he got a lot of other things, too. In sports, he is admired and idolized. Yet Russell says the Negro athlete cannot change public attitudes. Public attitudes HAVE changed. Just read Jackie Robinson's book. What was the public's attitude towards him before he came up? The truth was nobody wanted Negro athletes—no matter how good they were. Today they have been accepted and are a credit not only to their race but to the sports and the cities which they represent.

Under the exposure they receive, they've got to be more than stars. They've got to be gentlemen. Extra-special gentlemen. They've got to smile. They've got to be nice to the youngsters. Andy Johnson has always tried to do these things and he feels better because of it. One of Andy's teammates told this writer that "Andy Johnson is a feather in the cap of the Negro race." Quite a compliment, indeed.

As your writer, and having been associated with sports during my entire lifetime, I must wholeheartedly agree that Andy Johnson is among the finest gentlemen in sports today and I am justly proud to have had the privilege of knowing him and calling him FRIEND.

1

ABOVE: The French had a word for it — "Magnifique!" At least, this group of boys seems to think so as they watch the ball-handling technique of the Globetrotters during an afternoon game in Rouen.

ABOVE: Youngsters of all ages at Genoa, Italy, part of a crowd of 10,000 attending a one-night showing there, howl as the Trotters put on their famous comedy "circle".

'ROUND THE WORLD *kids are the same!*

ABOVE: Owner-coach Abe Saperstein of the Harlem Globetrotters satisfies the autograph fans after a game in Dortmund, Germany.

RIGHT: A quintet of blond Austrian youngsters, part of a crowd of 18,000 who attended a morning game in Vienna, laugh at the antics of the Harlem Globetrotters.

14

"The Truth is..."

I AM GOING TO SHARE SOME TRUTHS about my father's life that not only provide evidence for these words, but also reflect the stories of many African-American men who played professional basketball during the fifties and sixties. In many cases, you could substitute any one of their names for Dad's and these truths would be just as accurate.

Truth #1

Andy Johnson attended high school and college but rarely went to class. Andy Johnson did not graduate from high school, yet he was recruited and enrolled in an ambiguous degree program at Portland University. He was encouraged to skip class and to focus on playing basketball in order to bring home championships and fill the seats of gymnasiums and arenas.

Truth #2

Andy Johnson played for the Original Harlem Globetrotters and while enduring a challenging and often grueling schedule, he excelled as one of the top players the organization has ever known and served as a mentor to many of basketball's greats. Yet he also received low pay at the hands of the organization's leadership and demeaning treatment by an American system that did not believe his ability to make a successful living by playing basketball afforded him the chance to be treated equally, because of the color of his skin.

Truth #3

Andy Johnson was sold to the NBA's Philadelphia Warriors and was forced to surrender his natural scoring ability to the politics of keeping select other players on the team on top. He was later "loaned" to the Chicago Packers, where his skills were finally allowed to flourish, but found that his association with Abe Saperstein effectively ended his career.

Truth #4

Andy Johnson was blackballed out of the NBA after they promised to put him on waivers upon his release from Chicago, yet he never received the waiver. That injustice later affected his ability to gain access to his retroactive pension and severely stunted his professional basketball career.

Truth #5

I, Andy Johnson's son, wrote to the Coca-Cola Corporation to inquire about their very first print advertisement in an overseas country. They said that the first overseas print advertising campaign that they have archived includes photos of the Harlem Globetrotters (with Andy Johnson) overseas in the

One of the first Coca-Cola ads that circulated overseas. Dad and his teammates never received any monetary compensation, unlike today's athletes, who sometimes make more from their endorsements than what their sport provides. (Right to left): JC Gibson, Clarence Wilson, Bob "Showboat" Hall, Charlie Primus, Andy Johnson, and Ernest Wagner.

1950s. To my knowledge, no Harlem Globetrotter, including my father, has ever received compensation or royalties for that ad or any other ads. (Some of today's athletes often make more money in endorsements than they do in their salaries.)

Truth #6

Several years after Andy Johnson was forced out of the NBA and had completed his stint in the Eastern League, he searched for a job. I contacted a prominent Philadelphia sports figure and radio talk-show host, who had actually hung around the Warrior locker room waiting for a chance to see my dad after games and who solicited Dad's help in championing various charity events in the community.

I had hoped that my dad's reputation of being a man of good character and his assistance in helping this person rise to the status that he'd reached in sports (even though he'd never actually played in the NBA) would at least garner Dad a minor administrative or coaching position—something that allowed him to be around basketball—especially considering the major contacts the individual had. Unfortunately, this "prominent" person thought Andy Johnson was only worthy of a job in a warehouse.

When I called back to try to understand his selection of jobs, he simply said it was over for Andy Johnson and hung up the phone. Yet, whenever he's interviewed about the Great Andy Johnson, he touts Andy as being one of the best ballplayers to ever play the game. I guess the reality is that fans are sometimes unstable and ungrateful.

Truth #7

I am glad the NBA Hall of Fame finally recognized the contribution that was made by the Harlem Globetrotters—but how can you induct an *entire team* into the Basketball Hall of Fame when there were so many great players? That's like inducting the entire NBA into the Hall of Fame. It would have been better if the NBA had established a special division for the Trotters; that way all of the great Trotters would finally get the recognition that they deserve.

Truth #8
The Harlem Globetrotters never gave any of these phenomenal players a pension. Owner Mannie Jackson has donated millions to the NBA Hall of Fame and humanitarian causes. He simply seems to have forgotten to honor and create something for the the guys who paved the way for him and the organization.

Truth #9
In 1952, Alfred Palca was an idealistic film-maker, as well as a bit of a sports nut. He created the story of Abe Saperstein and the Harlem Globetrotters. The movie was *Go Man Go*, starring Sidney Poitier, which was partly responsible for the success overseas before the Harlem Globetrotters arrived.

Palca, with left wing leanings, was viewed as subversive. Indeed, the motion picture industry went so far as to create a Blacklist of people suspected of having Communist leanings.

The only way he could finish the movie and arrange for its distribution in theaters was to remove his name from the credits. *Go Man Go* did get released but without a mention of Palca's name.

Palca's filmmaking career never really revived after he was Blacklisted. But he never lost his belief that people of all races and religious backgrounds could live together in harmony.

These are facts. Anyone can make the same phone calls I did, talk to the same people I did, and get the same answers.

A record crowd of close to 22,000 at Chicago stadium on Nov. 29, 1940

EPILOGUE
The Final Shot

THIS STORY IS NOT JUST ABOUT MY DAD, Andy Johnson. No, this book is about a professional basketball player, who by most accounts was one of the greatest the sport has ever seen. It's about his labor through the birth pains of a profession that many young African American "ballers" take for granted now.

To effectively understand basketball today, it's incredibly important to learn about those people, like my father, who blazed the trail filled with a multitude of obstacles, setbacks, discouragements, and complications and made it possible for today's average players to sit on the bench while earning a million dollars or more a year—an amount of money my dad and his colleagues never made in their lifetimes.

Dad used to say, "Those are old skeletons that these young NBA players are running up and down the court on." Which was his unique way of stating that the Russells, Jordans, Iversons, and Lebrons were standing on the shoulders of the Pop Gates, Goose Tatums, "Sweet Waters", Hank DeZonis, and many other greats. And of course, his own.

When I heard that NBA superstar Shaquille O'Neal reached out to the family of George Mikan, an NBA player from the pre-1965 era, and assisted them during their hardships by paying for the legend's funeral, I was elated. In addition to adding fuel to the discussions about the NBA's treatment of the older players' pensions, Shaq also has made it possible for more NBA players of today to step up to the plate and recognize the importance of these older players, especially since the NBA/ Globetrotter organizations seems to be ambivalent, at best.

This story had to be told—a real "Hoop Dreams" from the life of one who lived it. Dad shared a substantial part of the lives of some of the greatest basketball players that ever lived— and yet, as he got older, he longed for the education he felt was denied him.

"Now I think I would give up basketball for a degree in school. People dream of playing ball. I dream of being able to spell like others can."—Andy Johnson

Andy Johnson felt strongly about the role of education in a person's life, and he would want people to learn from his story. He always said, "They can take your car, house, and money away from you, but they can't take your mind from you."

"They" can represent anything or anyone that impedes your ability to maximize your mind in any area of your life. "They" can be bad relationships, drugs, alcohol—anything. No matter what, Dad wanted people to know they truly can do anything they set their minds to do. He believed wholeheartedly that if you keep the right state of mind, you can make it.

Dad did what he wanted to do. It may not have been *where* he wanted to do it or *how* he wanted to do it, but he did it. He played basketball. He stayed in the game. And that was the most important thing for Dad in basketball and in life, to walk away from both standing straight, knowing that he *stayed in the game.*

He never turned to vices such as drugs and alcohol to take him out of the game of life. You can never score if you're on the bench, and that is what these things do to you.

I loved him. Too many people never develop a relationship with their fathers. I got a chance to do that, which makes getting his story out that much more urgent.

My dad's best Army buddy, Bruce McLeod, who was supposed to fly to visit Dad the day the 9/11 tragedy occurred, so eloquently said in a letter following my dad's death that Dad would not want *my heart to linger long in memory of days gone.* Andy Johnson would tell me to get on with living the rest of my life, to "be strong and of good courage."

So, writing this book *is* probably as much about healing for me as it is about sharing my father's legacy and enlightening future athletes about basketball's complicated history.

I know he would be proud, because I am.

Appendix A
Writings and Sayings of Andy Johnson

DESPITE HIS LIMITED FORMAL EDUCATION, Dad loved to write down his ideas and philosophies. Following are a few of the thoughts I was able to decipher from his journals. He loved to discuss relationships, particularly the issue of domestic violence (he saw it around him as an athlete). Maybe in another life, he would have been a psychologist.

#1

In a relationship, how much of the other person do you own? When a person says, "I want to be in a relationship," how much of themselves are they willing to give up? If you think you own a part of that person, how much are you willing to pay for it, if the person is willing to sell? If nobody is willing to sell, there is nothing to buy and it becomes a free relationship. In a free relationship, you love someone and demand no love in return.

Who do you think you are, that you can create a person? Who do you think you are that you can make a person to your likeness, make ears that only hear you, eyes that only see you, a mind that only thinks of you, and a brain that only knows what you say? Is that the reason the hitting started?

The most dangerous thing in the world is a bad relationship between a man and woman. When the fire of love goes out and it cannot make you warm anymore, then it's time to try to light it up again. If you cannot light it up in a peaceful way, then it's time to start working on you. It could have been because of you that the war started. You have to step back and look before you hit. Look into the mirror of your soul before you start blaming the other person, because you could have been the cause of all causes. Instead of hitting, go away and work on you. You cannot beat the fire of love into another person. As long as you blame the other person for your unhappiness, you will find yourself on a road with no turnoffs.

In order for the truth to be complete, it takes one to speak it and one to hear it.

The truth doesn't need a crutch, it stands by itself.

One of God's blessings is to be able to act your age.

Who can be satisfied without sacrifice?

If you want to be seen, you better know what you're showing.

Some people know all things except their own ignorance.

What right do you have to be mad at someone because they won't allow you to dream for them?

Don't feel bad if people don't recognize you for who you are, because God said, "I was in the world, created the world, and the world knew me not."

Trying to be a different person than what you are shows people what you never were.

In what year did women figure out that having a baby don't make a man do anything?

Who do you think you are that says, "I am the greatest?"

I ask the surgeon, "If you can make the incision, why can't you heal it?"

I ask the pathologist, "If you can tell the cause of death, why can't you stop it?"

I ask the psychiatrist, "If you can study the mind, why can't you read it?"

I ask the scientist, "If you can study man, why can't you make one?"

I ask the mathematician, "Give me the cost of the sun and the moon at today's electric prices."

I ask the lawyer, "How would you plead the devil's case before the throne of God?"

I ask you, "Who is the greatest?"

#2

If you try to bring another person down, you might fall down yourself. Each time you tried to bring me down, I grew taller. Each time you lied to me, I got closer to the truth. Each time you tried to make me deal with hate, I became closer to love. Each time you tried to make me into something I was not, I came closer to myself. Each time you tried to put the devil on me, I grew closer to God. The hands on their body is the only weapon another person can use against you. If you can control their hands, you take away the only weapon another person can use.

Some people think they are doing you a favor by letting you be in their company. Most mothers teach their daughters, from little on up, how pretty they are and how they can get any man they want. The man's reward is being with her, as long as he does what she says. Some mothers never teach their daughters that looks aren't everything. Some mothers never teach their daughters how to be nice, courteous, and kind. They never teach her that looks won't make you happy and you can't be right all the time. Be who you are from day one. Don't put on a show. Tell him your likes and dislikes, wants and needs up front, so there are no misunderstandings. If you put on a show when you first meet and then change back to who you really are, the shock might be too great for the other person and that's when the fighting starts. Then they try to beat into you the person they thought you were.

How much man is your woman?

Women are two people in one. You are who you act like: one who can't take "no" for an answer; an unruly person that thinks that they are better than anyone they might come in contact with. Some women think the man in them is more man than the man they are living with. Maybe it's the male hormones in their medications that make them think they are more male than female. Some women play both roles because the father of their children is not in the household. They play the male so long that it's hard for them to get back to the female side of themselves. When another man comes into their life, they don't understand what's happening and that's when the abuse starts. He thinks he's hitting the man in her. Her mouth tells him she's a man. When you hit the man in her, you are hitting the woman, too, though. When the man goes to court, he will lose because he cannot explain to the judge that he was hitting the man that came out of her.

Appendix B
African Americans in the NBA

THE NATIONAL BASKETBALL ASSOCIATION started with sixteen teams in the 1950s. After the first ten years, only eight teams remained. The unwritten rule was that no NBA team could have more than two black players. Not all of the teams exercised their rights to have blacks on their team. Most of the franchises that chose not to have blacks on their teams folded within a few years.

PIONEERS ASSOCIATED WITH THE NBL
BEFORE 1950
Frank Washington—Washington Bears
Bill Farrow—Youngstown Bears
Pop Gates—Tri-City Hawks
Bill Jones—Toledo

THESE ARE THE PIONEERS, BOTH TEAMS
AND PLAYERS

1950-51 Season, 4 new players
Earl Lloyd—Washington Capitals
Hank DeZonie—Tri Cities Blackhawks
Chuck Cooper—Boston Celtics
Nat "Sweetwater" Clifton—New York Knicks

1951-52 Season, 3 new players, 5 total players
Don Barksdale—Baltimore Bullets—Second leading scorer
Chuck Cooper—Boston Celtics
Nat Clifton—New York Knicks—Rebound stats

1952-53 Season, 0 new players, 6 total players
Don Barksdale—Baltimore Bullets
Chuck Cooper—Boston Celtics
Nat "Sweetwater" Clifton—New York Knicks—Rebound stats
Earl Lloyd—Syracuse Nationals

1953-54 Season, 1 new player, 5 total players
Ray Felix—Baltimore Bullets—Leading scorer/Rebound stats
Don Barksdale—Boston Celtics
Chuck Cooper—Boston Celtics
Nat "Sweetwater" Clifton – New York Knicks
Earl Lloyd—Syracuse Nationals

1954-55 Season, 3 new players, 9 total players
Don Barksdale—Boston Celtics
Chuck Cooper—Milwaukee Hawks
Ray Felix—New York Knicks
Nat "Sweetwater" Clifton—New York Knicks
Jackie Moore—Philadelphia Warriors

Earl Lloyd—Syracuse Nationals
Jim Tucker—Syracuse Nationals

1955-1956 Season, 3 new players, 9 total players

Ray Felix—New York Knicks
Nat "Sweetwater" Clifton—New York Knicks
Walter Dukes—New York Knicks
Jackie Moore – Philadelphia Warriors
Maurice Stokes—Rochester Royals
Earl Lloyd—Syracuse Nationals
Jim Tucker—Syracuse Nationals
Ed Fleming—Rochester Royals

1956-1957 Season, 6 new players, 14 total players

Bill Russell—Boston Celtics
Walter Dukes—Minnesota Lakers
Ray Felix—New York Knicks
Nat "Sweetwater" Clifton—New York Knicks
Willie Naulls—New York Knicks
Jackie Moore—Philadelphia Warriors
Maurice Stokes—Rochester Royals—Rebound stats
Dick Ricketts—Rochester Royals
Sihugo Green—Rochester Royals
Earl Lloyd—Syracuse Nationals
Bob Hopkins-Syracuse Nationals
Jim Tucker—Syracuse Nationals
Bob Williams—Minnesota Lakers
Hal Lear—Philadelphia Warriors
Ed Fleming—Rochester Royals

1957-1958 Season, 3 new players, 11 total players

Bill Russell—Boston Celtics—Rebound stats/score stats

Sam Jones—Boston Celtics
Maurice Stokes—Cincinnati Royals -Rebound stats
Dick Ricketts—Cincinnati Royals
Walter Dukes—Detroit Pistons—Rebound stats
Nat "Sweetwater" Clifton—Detroit Pistons
Willie Nauls—New York Knicks—Rebound stats/score stats
Ray Felix—New York Knicks
Woody Sauldsberry—Philadelphia Warriors
Bob Hopkins—Syracuse Nationals
Earl Lloyd—Syracuse Nationals
Ed Flemng—Minneapolis Lakers

1958-1959 Season, 4 new players, 15 total players
Bill Russell—Boston Celtics—Rebound stats
Sam Jones—Boston Celtics—
KC Jones—Boston Celtics
Walter Dukes—Detroit Pistons
Earl Lloyd—Detroit Pistons
Elgin Baylor—Minneapolis Lakers
Willie Nauls – New York Knicks
Ray Felix—New York Knicks
Woody Sauldsberry—Philadelphia Warriors
Guy Rodgers—Philadelphia Warriors
Andy Johnson—Philadelphia Warriors
Sihugo Green—St. Louis Hawks
Hal Greer—Syracuse Nationals
Bob Hopkins—Syracuse Nationals
Ed Flemng—Minneapolis Lakers

1959-1960 Season, 2 new players, 18 total players
Bill Russell—Boston Celtics

Sam Jones—Boston Celtics
KC Jones—Boston Celtics
Walter Dukes—Detroit Pistons
Earl Lloyd—Detroit Pistons
Elgin Baylor—Minnesota Lakers
Ray Felix—Minnesota Lakers
Willie Naulls—New York Knicks
Cal Ramsey—New York Knicks
Wilt Chamberlain—Philadelphia Warriors
Guy Rodgers—Philadelphia Warriors
Woody Sauldsberry—Philadelphia Warriors
Andy Johnson—Philadelphia Warriors
Sihugo Green—St. Louis Hawks
Hal Greer—Syracuse Nationals
Dick Barnett—Syracuse Nationals
Bob Hopkins—Syracuse Nationals
Ed Flemng—Minneapolis Lakers

1960-1961 Season, 4 new players, 19 total players
Bill Russell—Boston Celtics
KC Jones—Boston Celtics
Sam Jones—Boston Celtics
Oscar Robertson—Cincinnati Royals
Walter Dukes—Detroit Pistons
Elgin Baylor—Los Angeles Lakers
Ray Felix—Los Angeles Lakers
Willie Naulls—New York Knicks
Wilt Chamberlain—Philadelphia Warriors
Guy Rodgers—Philadelphia Warriors
Andy Johnson—Philadelphia Warriors
Al Attles—Philadelphia Warriors

LennyWilkens—St. Louis Hawks
Sihugo Green—St. Louis Hawks
Woody Sauldsbury—St. Louis Hawks
Fred LaCour—St. Louis Hawks
Hal Greer—Syracuse Nationals
Dick Barnett—Syracuse Nationals
Cal Ramsey—Syracuse Nationals

1961-1962 Season, 2 new players, 12 total players
Bill Russell—Boston Celtics
Sam Jones—Boston Celtics
KC Jones—Boston Celtics
Walt Bellamy—Chicago Packers
Andy Johnson—Chicago Packers
Sihugo Green—Chicago Packers
Woody Saulsbury—Chicago Packers
Oscar Roberson—Cincinnati Royals
Joe Buckhalter—Cincinnati Royals

PIONEERS DURING THE ERA OF PROFESSIONALISM. MOST EITHER PLAYED FOR THE HARLEM RENS OR THE HARLEM GLOBTROTTERS BEFORE 1950.

Puggy Bell
Zack Clayton
Tarzan Cooper
Hank Dezonie
Bill Farrow
Eddie Younger
George Grave
Mark Hannibal

Marquis Haynes
Charles Isles
Bill Jones
William
"Dolly" King
Tony Peyton
Fran Robinson
Pablo Robinson

Eyue Saitch
Tom Sealy
Sidal Sing
Wie Wille Smith
Jim Usry
Rabbit Warthu

Some of the best amateur teams of the time:

The Smart Set Athletic Club of Brooklyn, St. Christopher Club of New York City, Marathon Athletic Club of Brooklyn, Crescent Athletic Club, The Twelfth Street Colored YMCA of Washington, DC, Monticello Athletic Association and the Wabash Avenue Colored YMCA "Outlaws were Spartan Braves and Spartan Hornets

This list was compiled through my research, and is a complete list to my knowledge. If I have for forgotten anyone, I truly apologize.

Top: The Harlem Renaissance, bottom: The Savoy Big Five, right: The Commonwealth Five.

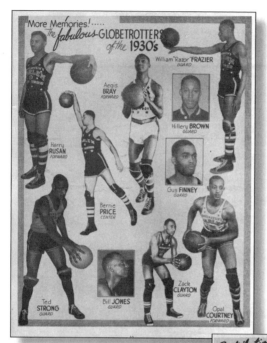

Harry Rusan, Bernie Price,
Aegis Bray, William "Razor"
Frazier, Hillery Brown,
Gus Finney, Ted Strong,
Bill Jones, Zack Clayton,
Opal Courtney

Reece "Goose" Tatum, Sam Sharpe,
Al Price, Bruce Wright, "Pop" Gates,
Roscoe Julien, Sonny Boswell

Donald "Ducky" Moore,
Everett Marcell, Roosevelt Hudson,
Roscoe "Duke" Cumberland,
Ermer Robinson, Louis "Babe" Pressley,
Lorenzo "Piper" Davis